The

Griswold Mfg. Co.
ERIE, PA

Catalog No. 47
REPRINT

Reprinted in 1996

with 1996 price guide

L-W Book Sales
P.O. Box 69
Gas City, IN 46933

Introduction

This is a copy of the original 1918 Catalog from Griswold, including 1996 prices. What better way to identify and date your Griswold Collection?

PRICING NOTE

The current prices as listed in this book should only be used as a guide. Prices will vary from one region of the country to another, dealers' prices vary greatly and are affected by condition as well as demand. These prices were gathered from different auctions, antique shows, and flea markets and are subject to change. The publisher assumes no responsiblity for any gains or losses that may be incurred as a result of consulting this guide.

Acknowledgments

We would like to give a special thank you to Gwen Goldman for finding this great catalog for us. We believe you will enjoy her great find tremendously. Thank you Gwen!!!

GWEN GOLDMAN

for all your paper collectible needs!

P.O. Box 936
Adamstown, PA 19501
717-484-0487

Table of Contents

MARVIN E. GRISWOLD, Prest.
ELY GRISWOLD, Vice Prest.

MATTHEW GRISWOLD, Chairman

M. W. GRISWOLD, Secy & Treas.
JOHN L. HOLLANDER, Sales Mgr.

May 18, 1918.
WEDNESDAY

Hardware Mnfrs' Organization
for War Service,
1218 New York, Ave., N. W.,
Washington, D. C.

Attention Mr. Murray Sargent

My Dear Mr. Sargent:

We enclose herewith copy of our
catalogue, and wish that you could have this
properly listed with the Bureau of Supplies and
Accounts, so if the Government is in need of any
thing in this line, they would send us the bidding
blanks.

Yours very truly,

MEG-M

THE GRISWOLD MNFG. CO.

Original Letter signed by
Marvin E. Griswold, Vice President

CAST
ALUMINUM
WARE

BULLETIN
NUMBER A-9

THE GRISWOLD MFG. CO.
ERIE, PENNSYLVANIA, U. S. A.

TERMS.

Sixty days or two per cent discount for cash if paid within 10 days from date of invoice.

All bills payable in New York or other par funds without allowance for exchange.

No charge for crating or cartage.

No freight allowance on shipments weighing less than 200 pounds. Positively no deviation from this rule.

We take special care in the packing of our goods. Every piece is carefully packed, insuring against breakage.

After goods are shipped in good order our liability ceases, and we cannot allow any claims for breakage or other damage in transit.

Claims for errors or deficiencies will not be entertained unless made within FIVE DAYS after receipt of goods.

THE REASONS WHY "GRISWOLD" TEMPERED CAST PURE ALUMINUM COOKING UTENSILS ARE THE BEST.

FIRST. They are light in weight, bright as silver, and absolutely pure and wholesome.

SECOND. They are solid metal throughout, there being no enamel or plating to flake or wear off.

THIRD. They will not burn or scorch food as readily as other metals.

FOURTH. They conduct heat more rapidly than other metals and retain it longer.

FIFTH. They do not contain or form any of the poisonous substances found in tin, copper or enameled ware.

SIXTH. There are no joints, seams, rivets or solder to leak and give trouble. Cast in one piece, are thicker and stronger, and will outlast any other ware.

SEVENTH. All inside polished surfaces have a special hard tempered finish which does not discolor easily.

CAST ALUMINUM WARE
Tempered

COFFEE POT

Cat. No.	Capacity. Quarts.	Height. Inches.	List Price. Each.
101	1	6	$3.20
102	2	7	3.50
103	3	8	3.85
104	4	9	4.30

TEA POT

Cat. No.	Capacity. Quarts.	Height. Inches.	List Price. Each.
111	1	6	$3.45
112	2	7	3.75
113	3	8	4.15
114	4	9	4.60

CAST ALUMINUM WARE
Tempered

COFFEE PER=KO=LA=TOR

Cat. No.	Capacity. Cups.	Capacity. Pints.	Height. Inches. Over Glass Top.	List Price. Each.
176	6	2	$9\frac{9}{16}$	**$6.50**
179	9	3	$10\frac{5}{16}$	**7.00**
1713	13	$4\frac{1}{2}$	11	**7.50**

Cut showing the simple and quick pumping device Seamless Pot. CAST IN ONE PIECE. Nothing to get out of order or come apart.

CAST ALUMINUM WARE
Tempered

TEA POT

Cat. No.	Capacity. Pints.	List Price. Each.
132	2	$3.30
133	3	3.70
134	4	4.10

FIVE O'CLOCK TEA KETTLE

Cat. No.	Capacity. Pints.	List Price. Each.
152	2	$3.30
153	3	3.70
154	4	4.10

CAST ALUMINUM WARE

DOUBLE BOILER

Cat. No.	Capacity. Quarts.	Diameter. Inches.	List Price. Each.
401	1	$6\frac{3}{4}$	$2.75
402	2	$7\frac{3}{4}$	3.50
403	3	$8\frac{3}{4}$	4.40
404	4	$9\frac{3}{4}$	5.15

Stamped Aluminum inside dish and cover. Cast outside dish made extra large to hold plenty of water, to prevent boiling dry.

COLONIAL DESIGN FLAT BOTTOM TEA KETTLE

Cat. No.	Trade No.	Capacity. Quarts.	Dia. Bottom. Inches.	List Price. Each.
532	4	2	$7\frac{1}{8}$	$3.00
533	5	3	$7\frac{3}{4}$	3.30
534	6	4	$8\frac{7}{8}$	3.60
535	7	5	$9\frac{1}{2}$	3.95
536	8	6	$9\frac{3}{4}$	4.25
538	9	8	10	4.75

Each Tea Kettle full capacity as rated. Compare our trade number, capacity and quality with other Cast Aluminum Tea Kettles.

CAST ALUMINUM WARE

"SAFETY FIRST" COLONIAL TEA KETTLE

Cat. No.	Trade No.	Capacity. Quarts.	Dia. Bottom. Inches.	List Price. Each.
546	8	6	$9\frac{3}{4}$	$4.75

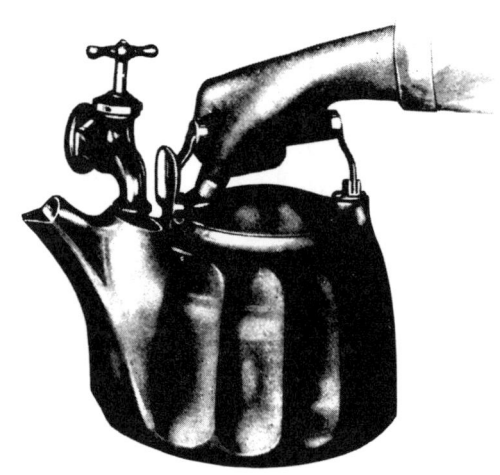

Patented

The newest and best in Tea Kettle construction. Can be filled under any faucet, without the steam burning the hand.

Note the extra large bottom.

CAST ALUMINUM WARE

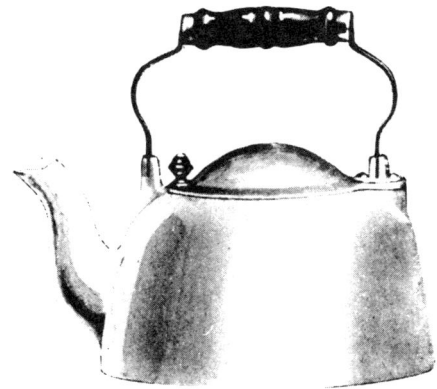

FLAT BOTTOM TEA KETTLE

Cat. No.	Trade. No.	Capacity. Quarts.	Dia. Bottom. Inches.	List Price. Each.
512	4	2	$7\frac{1}{8}$	$3.00
513	5	3	$7\frac{3}{4}$	3.30
514	6	4	$8\frac{7}{8}$	3.60
515	7	5	$9\frac{3}{4}$	3.95
516	8	6	10	4.25
518	9	8	11	4.75

"THE RAPID" CORRUGATED BOTTOM TEA KETTLE

Cat. No.	Trade No.	Capacity.		Dia. Bottom. Inches.	List Price. Each.
$501\frac{1}{2}$	4	$3\frac{1}{2}$	Pts	$5\frac{3}{4}$	$2.85
$502\frac{1}{2}$	5	5	"	$6\frac{5}{8}$	3.10
504	6	4	Qts	$7\frac{3}{8}$	3.60
505	7	5	"	$8\frac{1}{2}$	3.95
506	8	6	"	$9\frac{1}{8}$	4.25
508	9	8	"	$9\frac{3}{4}$	4.75

CAST ALUMINUM WARE

WATER PITCHER

Cat. No.	Capacity. Quarts.	List Price Each.
165	$2\frac{1}{2}$	$3.50

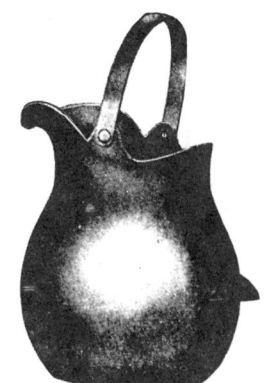

BAIL WATER PITCHER

For Bell Boy use in Hotels

Cat. No.	Capacity. Quarts.	List Price. Each.
172	$2\frac{1}{2}$	$3.50

CAST ALUMINUM WARE
Tempered

SKILLET
Wood Handle

Cat. No.	Trade No.	Diameter, Inches.	Depth. Inches.	List Price. Each.
203	3	$6\frac{1}{2}$	$1\frac{1}{4}$	$1.40
204	4	$6\frac{7}{8}$	$1\frac{1}{2}$	1.55
205	5	8	$1\frac{7}{8}$	1.70
206	6	9	2	1.85
207	7	$9\frac{3}{4}$	$2\frac{1}{4}$	1.95
208	8	$10\frac{1}{2}$	$2\frac{1}{4}$	2.15
209	9	$11\frac{1}{2}$	$2\frac{1}{4}$	2.45
2010	10	12	$2\frac{1}{4}$	3.25
2011	11	$12\frac{1}{2}$	$2\frac{1}{4}$	3.50
2012	12	$13\frac{1}{4}$	$2\frac{1}{4}$	4.10

SKILLET
With Iron Tinned Handle

Cat. No.	Trade No.	Diameter. Inches.	Depth. Inches.	List Price. Each.
215	5	8	$1\frac{7}{8}$	$1.70
216	6	9	2	1.85
217	7	$9\frac{3}{4}$	$2\frac{1}{4}$	1.95
218	8	$10\frac{1}{2}$	$2\frac{1}{4}$	2.15
219	9	$11\frac{1}{2}$	$2\frac{1}{4}$	2.45
2110	10	12	$2\frac{1}{4}$	3.25
2111	11	$12\frac{1}{2}$	$2\frac{1}{4}$	3.50
2112	12	$13\frac{1}{4}$	$2\frac{1}{4}$	4.10

CAST ALUMINUM WARE
Tempered

SHALLOW SKILLET

Cat. No.	Trade No.	Diameter. Inches.	Depth. Inches.	List Price. Each.
227	7	9	$\frac{3}{4}$	$1.80
228	8	$9\frac{13}{16}$	$\frac{3}{4}$	1.90
229	9	11	1	2.10
2210	10	$12\frac{3}{8}$	$1\frac{1}{4}$	2.50

OYSTER PAN

Cat. No.	Capacity. Pints.	Diameter. Inches.	Depth. Inches.	LIST PRICE EACH Without Cover.	With Cover.	Cover No.
232	2	$7\frac{3}{4}$	2	$1.75	$2.20	499

CAST ALUMINUM WARE

Tempered

HANDLE GRIDDLE

Cat. No.	Trade No.	Diameter. Top Inches.	List Price. Each.
306	6	$7\frac{1}{8}$	$1.60
307	7	8	1.80
308	8	9	2.00
309	9	$10\frac{3}{8}$	2.35
3010	10	$11\frac{1}{4}$	2.75

BAILED GRIDDLE

Cat. No.	Trade No.	Diameter. Top Inches.	List Price. Each.
3110	10	10	$2.10
3112	12	$11\frac{5}{16}$	2.50
3114	14	$13\frac{3}{4}$	3.20

CAST ALUMINUM WARE
Tempered

LONG GRIDDLE

Cat. No.	Trade No.	Length. Inches.	Width. Inches.	List Price. Each.
327	7	$16\frac{1}{2}$	$7\frac{1}{4}$	$2.90
328	8	19	$8\frac{1}{2}$	3.70
329	9	21	$9\frac{5}{8}$	5.25
3210	10	$24\frac{1}{2}$	$12\frac{1}{2}$	6.50

Long Griddle Bailed List 20 cents additional.

BERLIN SAUCE PAN
Side Handle

Cat. No.	Capacity. Quarts.	Diameter. Inches.	Depth. Inches.	LIST PRICE EACH. Without Cover.	With Cover.	Cover No.
$442\frac{1}{2}$	$2\frac{1}{2}$	$6\frac{1}{2}$	$4\frac{3}{4}$	$2.85	$3.15	$442\frac{1}{2}$ C
444	4	$7\frac{1}{4}$	$5\frac{1}{4}$	3.20	3.65	444 C
445	5	8	$5\frac{1}{2}$	3.85	4.30	445 C
446	6	$8\frac{1}{2}$	6	4.40	4.90	446 C
447	7	9	$6\frac{1}{2}$	4.90	5.45	447 C
4410	10	10	$7\frac{1}{2}$	5.55	6.25	4410 C

CAST ALUMINUM WARE
Tempered

BERLIN BOILER

Cat. No.	Capacity. Quarts.	Diameter. Inches.	Depth. Inches.	LIST PRICE EACH. Without Cover.	With Cover.	Cover No.
422½	2½	6½	4¾	$2.70	$3.00	422½C
424	4	7¼	5¼	3.05	3.50	424 C
425	5	8	5½	3.70	4.20	425 C
426	6	8½	6	4.10	4.65	426 C
427	7	9	6½	4.60	5.20	427 C
4210	10	10	7½	5.30	6.00	4210 C

BERLIN SAUCE PAN

Cat. No.	Capacity. Quarts.	Diameter. Inches.	Depth. Inches.	LIST PRICE EACH. Without Cover.	With Cover.	Cover No.
432½	2½	6½	4¾	$2.85	$3.15	432½C
434	4	7¼	5¼	3.20	3.65	434 C
435	5	8	5½	3.85	4.30	435 C
436	6	8½	6	4.40	4.90	436 C
437	7	9	6½	4.90	5.45	437 C
4310	10	10	7½	5.55	6.25	4310 C

CAST ALUMINUM WARE

Tempered

SAUCE PAN WITH LIP

Cat. No.	Capacity. Quarts.	Diameter. Inches.	Depth. Inches.	LIST PRICE EACH. Without Cover.	With Cover.	Cover No.
412	2	$7\frac{3}{4}$	$4\frac{1}{4}$	$2.30	$2.80	412C
413	3	$8\frac{1}{2}$	$4\frac{3}{4}$	2.60	3.15	413C
414	4	9	5	2.90	3.50	414C

BUFFET SAUCE PAN WITH LIP

Cat. No.	Capacity. Pints.	Diameter. Inches.	Depth. Inches.	LIST PRICE EACH. Without Cover.	With Cover.	Cover No.
411	2	6	$2\frac{1}{2}$	$1.60	$1.90	411 C
$411\frac{1}{2}$	3	$7\frac{1}{2}$	3	1.80	2.25	$411\frac{1}{2}$C

CAST ALUMINUM WARE
Tempered

FLAT BOTTOM KETTLE

Cat. No.	Trade No.	Capacity. Quarts.	Dia. Top. Inches.	LIST PRICE EACH. Without Cover.	With Cover.	Cover No.
474	6	4	$8\frac{1}{4}$	$2.95	$3.30	474C
476	7	6	$9\frac{1}{4}$	3.35	3.75	476C
477	8	7	$9\frac{7}{8}$	3.90	4.35	477C
479	9	9	$10\frac{3}{4}$	4.95	5.45	479C

MASLIN KETTLE

Cat. No.	Capacity. Quarts.	Diameter. Inches.	Depth. Inches.	LIST PRICE EACH. Without Cover.	With Cover.	Cover No.
454	4	9	5	$2.70	$3.30	454C
456	6	10	$5\frac{5}{8}$	3.00	3.70	456C
458	8	$11\frac{1}{2}$	$6\frac{1}{2}$	4.00	4.80	458C
4512	12	$12\frac{3}{8}$	$7\frac{1}{2}$	5.60	6.60	4512C
4516	16	14	$7\frac{5}{8}$	8.50	9.50	4516C
4520	20	$14\frac{3}{4}$	$8\frac{5}{8}$	10.00	11.25	4520C
4524	24	$15\frac{1}{2}$	$9\frac{1}{2}$	12.00	13.50	4524C

CAST ALUMINUM WARE

Tempered

ROASTER OR DUTCH OVEN

Cat. No.	Trade No.	Capacity. Quarts.	Diameter. Inches.	List Price Each. With Cover.
462½	6	2½	8	$3.75
463½	7	3½	9	4.35
465	8	5	10	4.85
466	9	6	11	5.20
468	10	8	12½	6.75
4612	11	12	13½	8.05

OVAL ROASTER

Cat. No.	Trade No.	Size. Inches.	Depth. Inches.	List Price Each. With Cover.
483	3	8 x12	5	$5.25
485	5	9¼x14	6	6.85
487	7	11 x15¾	7	8.50

These Roasters have flat bottoms, high dome cast covers.

CAST ALUMINUM WARE

WAFFLE MOULD
American Pattern, Low Ring

Cat. No.	Trade No.	Diameter of Pan. Inches	Diameter Bottom of Ring. Inches	List Price. Each.
606	6	$5\frac{3}{4}$	8	$2.25
607	7	$6\frac{3}{4}$	$8\frac{3}{4}$	2.50
608	8	$7\frac{3}{4}$	$9\frac{7}{8}$	2.75
609	9	$8\frac{5}{8}$	$10\frac{5}{8}$	3.25

DEEP RING WAFFLE MOULD
American Pattern

Cat. No.	Trade No.	Shape.	Diameter of Pan. Inches	List Price Each.
617	7D	Round	$6\frac{3}{4}$	$2.75
618	8D	Round	$7\frac{3}{4}$	3.00
619	9D	Round	$8\frac{5}{8}$	3.50
6111	11	Square	$6\frac{3}{4}$x$6\frac{3}{4}$	3.00

Cast Aluminum Pans.   Iron japanned ring.
For Gas or Vapor Stoves.

CAST ALUMINUM WARE

SHIRRED EGG DISH

Cat. No.	Diameter. Inches.	Depth. Inches.	List Price Each.
56	6	$\frac{3}{4}$	$0.70

PUDDING PAN

Cat. No.	Capacity. Quarts.	Diameter. Inches.	Depth. Inches.	List Price Each.
191	1	$7\frac{1}{2}$	$2\frac{1}{4}$	$1.00
192	2	8	$2\frac{1}{2}$	1.65
$192\frac{1}{2}$	$2\frac{1}{2}$	8	$2\frac{3}{4}$	2.00
193	3	$10\frac{3}{4}$	$3\frac{1}{4}$	2.40
194	4	$11\frac{1}{4}$	$3\frac{1}{4}$	2.65

CASSEROLE

Tempered

Cat. No.	Capacity. Pints.	Diameter. Inches.	Depth. Inches.	List Price Each. With Cover.
182	2	$7\frac{1}{2}$	$2\frac{1}{8}$	$2.20
183	3	8	$2\frac{1}{2}$	2.60
184	4	$8\frac{1}{2}$	3	3.20

These Dishes have no seams nor joints. Note side handles.

CAST ALUMINUM WARE

OMELET FRY PAN
French Pattern

Cat. No.	Diameter. Inches.	Depth. Inches.	List Price. Each.
246	$6\frac{1}{2}$	$1\frac{1}{2}$	$1.00
247	$7\frac{1}{2}$	$1\frac{5}{8}$	1.30
249	$9\frac{1}{2}$	2	1.80
2411	$11\frac{1}{4}$	$2\frac{1}{4}$	2.50

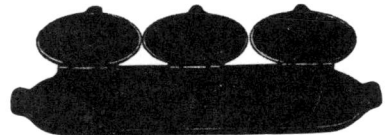

FLOP GRIDDLE

Cat. No.		List Price. Each.
338	3 Pans, 4 inches diameter	$2.50

BREAD STICK PAN

Cat. No.	Trade No.	Size. Inches.	CAKES. Size. Inches.	Depth. Inches.	List Price. Each.
8022	22	$13\frac{3}{8}$x$7\frac{3}{8}$	7x$1\frac{1}{8}$	$\frac{3}{4}$	$1.80

CAST ALUMINUM WARE

GEM OR MUFFIN PAN

Cat. No.	Trade No.	Size. Inches.	CAKES. Size. Inches.	Depth. Inches.	List Price. Each.
8017	17	$6\frac{7}{8}$x6	$1\frac{7}{8}$x3	$\frac{7}{8}$	$1.00

GEM OR MUFFIN PAN

Cat. No.	Trade No.	Size. Inches.	CAKES. Size. Inches.	Depth. Inches.	List Price. Each.
8016	16	7x7	2x$3\frac{1}{2}$	$1\frac{1}{8}$	$1.30

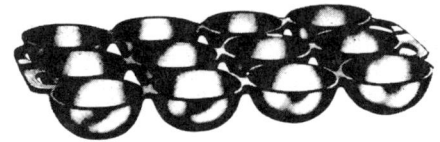

GOLF BALL GEM OR MUFFIN PAN

Cat. No.	Trade No.	Size. Inches.	CAKES. Diameter Inches.	Depth Inches.	List Price. Each.
809	9	$10\frac{3}{8}$x7	$2\frac{1}{8}$	1	$1.50

CAST ALUMINUM WARE

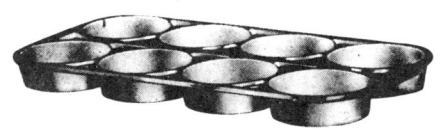

GEM OR MUFFIN PAN

Cat. No.	Trade No.	Size. Inches.	CAKES. Diameter. Inches.	Depth. Inches.	List Price. Each.
808	8	$12\frac{3}{4}$x$6\frac{3}{4}$	3	$\frac{7}{8}$	$1.50

GEM OR MUFFIN PAN

Cat. No.	Trade No.	Size. Inches.	CAKES. Size. Inches.	Depth. Inches.	List Price. Each.
8011	11	$11\frac{5}{8}$x6	3x$1\frac{1}{8}$	$\frac{7}{8}$	$1.50

GEM OR MUFFIN PAN

Cat. No.	Trade No.	Size. Inches.	No. of Cakes.	CAKES. Diam. Inches.	Depth. Inches.	List Price. Each.
8010	10	$10\frac{1}{2}$x$7\frac{1}{2}$	11	$2\frac{1}{2}$	$1\frac{3}{4}$	$2.00
8018	18	$7\frac{1}{2}$x5	6	$2\frac{1}{2}$	$1\frac{3}{4}$	1.25

EXTRA FINISHED IRON HOLLOW WARE

"ERIE"

BULLETIN
NUMBER E-5

THE GRISWOLD MFG. CO.
ERIE, PENNSYLVANIA, U. S. A.

TERMS.

Sixty days or two per cent. discount for cash if paid within 10 days from date of invoice.

All bills payable in New York or other par funds without allowance for exchange.

No charge for crating or cartage.

No freight allowance on shipments weighing less than 200 pounds. Positively no deviation from this rule.

We take special care in the packing of our goods. Every piece is wrapped in paper and carefully packed, insuring against breakage or rust.

After goods are shipped in good order our liability ceases, and we cannot allow any claims for breakage or other damage in transit.

Claims for errors or deficiencies will not be entertained unless made within FIVE DAYS after receipt of goods.

THE GRISWOLD EXTRA FINISHED IRON HOLLOW WARE is of the highest quality, and it cannot be made better.

Each piece is carefully moulded by experienced workmen, insuring thicker, heavier metal where durability and heat are required.

The choicest of high grade superior iron is used, making possible the highly polished surface. To preserve this finish each piece is VAPORIZED with a TRANSPARENT ANTI-RUST PREPARATION, which permits handling and eliminates the danger of rust from finger marks or atmospheric changes.

THE GRISWOLD is the only line of Extra Finished Ware made in which you are always sure of getting the best. Our ideas, like our wares, are original. Others may try to copy, but why not get the best, first and at all times. Look for our trade mark, our reputation is back of it.

EXTRA FINISHED IRON HOLLOW WARE

IRON HANDLE REGULAR SKILLET

No.	Dia. Top Inches	Dia. Bot. Inches	Depth Inches	Packed in Barrel	Wt. per Bbl. Pounds	Price List Polished	Price List Nick. Pltd.
3	$6\frac{1}{2}$	$5\frac{1}{4}$	$1\frac{1}{4}$	300	425	$ .34	$ .68
4	$6\frac{3}{4}$	$5\frac{1}{2}$	$1\frac{1}{2}$	175	425	.37	.74
5	8	$6\frac{3}{4}$	$1\frac{3}{4}$	140	420	.40	.80
6	$8\frac{7}{8}$	$7\frac{1}{2}$	2	120	425	.43	.86
7	$9\frac{5}{8}$	$8\frac{1}{4}$	$2\frac{1}{8}$	100	400	.46	.92
8	$10\frac{3}{8}$	$8\frac{7}{8}$	$2\frac{1}{4}$	90	410	.50	1.00
9	$11\frac{1}{4}$	$9\frac{3}{4}$	$2\frac{1}{4}$	75	410	.58	1.16
10	$11\frac{3}{4}$	$10\frac{1}{4}$	$2\frac{1}{4}$	68	420	.74	1.48
11	$12\frac{1}{2}$	$10\frac{7}{8}$	$2\frac{1}{4}$	60	425	.92	1.84
12	$13\frac{1}{4}$	$11\frac{3}{4}$	$2\frac{1}{4}$	55	440	1.10	2.20
13	14	$12\frac{1}{2}$	$2\frac{1}{4}$	48	450	1.30	2.60
14	$15\frac{1}{4}$	$13\frac{1}{2}$	$2\frac{1}{2}$	36	450	1.50	3.00

WOOD HANDLE SKILLET

No.	Dia. Top Inches	Dia. Bot. Inches	Depth Inches	Packed in Barrel	Wt. per Bbl. Pounds	Price List Polished	Price List Nick. Pltd.
3	$6\frac{1}{2}$	$5\frac{1}{4}$	$1\frac{1}{4}$	275	400	$ .49	$ .83
4	$6\frac{7}{8}$	$5\frac{1}{2}$	$1\frac{1}{2}$	250	425	.52	.89
5	8	$6\frac{3}{4}$	$1\frac{3}{4}$	120	340	.55	.95
6	$8\frac{7}{8}$	$7\frac{1}{2}$	2	100	325	.58	1.01
7	$9\frac{5}{8}$	$8\frac{1}{4}$	$2\frac{1}{8}$	80	340	.61	1.07
8	$10\frac{3}{8}$	$8\frac{7}{8}$	$2\frac{1}{4}$	72	330	.65	1.15
9	$11\frac{1}{4}$	$9\frac{3}{4}$	$2\frac{1}{4}$	60	340	.73	1.31
10	$11\frac{3}{4}$	$10\frac{1}{4}$	$2\frac{1}{4}$	50	330	.89	1.63
11	$12\frac{1}{4}$	$10\frac{3}{4}$	$2\frac{1}{2}$	45	340	1.07	1.99
12	13	12	$2\frac{1}{2}$	40	350	1.25	2.35

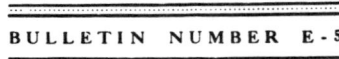
EXTRA FINISHED IRON HOLLOW WARE

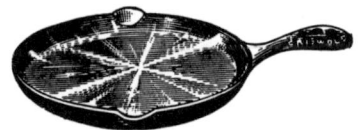

IRON HANDLE SHALLOW SKILLET

No.	Dia. Top Inches	Dia. Bot. Inches	Depth Inches	Packed in Barrel	Wt. per Bbl. Pounds	Price List Polished	Price List Nick. Pltd.
7	9	7	$\frac{3}{4}$	120	390	$ .42	$ .84
8	$9\frac{7}{8}$	$8\frac{3}{8}$	$\frac{3}{4}$	100	385	.46	.92
9	$11\frac{1}{16}$	9	1	90	400	.50	1.00
10	$12\frac{7}{8}$	$9\frac{1}{2}$	$1\frac{1}{4}$	70	390	.64	1.28

IRON HANDLE EXTRA DEEP SKILLET

No.	Dia. Top Inches	Dia. Bot. Inches	Depth Inches	Packed in Barrel	Wt. per Bbl. Pounds	Price List Polished	Price List Nick. Pltd
8	$10\frac{7}{8}$	9	3	70	420	$ .78	$1.56
9	$11\frac{7}{8}$	$9\frac{7}{8}$	3	60	410	.88	1.76
10	$12\frac{1}{4}$	$10\frac{1}{4}$	3	50	420	1.04	2.08

EXTRA FINISHED IRON HOLLOW WARE

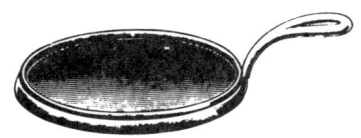

IRON HANDLE GRIDDLE

No.	Dia. Top Inches	Packed in Barrel	Wt. per Bbl. Pounds	Price List Polished	Price List Nickel Plated
6	$7\frac{1}{4}$	150	350	$ .32	$.64
7	8	120	360	.36	.72
8	$9\frac{1}{8}$	100	340	.40	.80
9	$10\frac{3}{8}$	100	425	.48	.96
10	$11\frac{7}{16}$	90	440	.62	1.24

WOOD HANDLE GRIDDLE

No.	Dia. Top Inches	Packed in Barrel	Wt. per Bbl. Pounds	Price List Polished	Price List Nickel Plated
6	7	125	320	$ .47	$ .79
7	8	100	340	.51	.87
8	$9\frac{1}{8}$	100	350	.55	.95
9	$10\frac{3}{8}$	80	330	.63	1.11
10	$11\frac{7}{16}$	75	340	.77	1.39

EXTRA FINISHED IRON HOLLOW WARE

BAILED GRIDDLE

No.	Dia. Top Inches	Packed in Barrel	Wt. per Bbl. Pounds	Price List Polished	Price List Nickel Plated
10	$10\frac{3}{4}$	60	340	$ .62	$1.24
12	12	50	330	.70	1.40
14	$14\frac{3}{8}$	40	340	.90	1.80
16	$16\frac{3}{16}$	36	375	1.10	2.20

New England

IRON HANDLE GRIDDLE

No.	Dia. Top Inches	Dia. Bot. Inches	Depth Inches	Packed in Barrel	Wt. per Bbl. Pounds	Price List Polished	Price List Nickel Plated
8=NE	9	7	$\frac{11}{16}$	150	350	$ .40	$ .80
9=NE	$9\frac{3}{4}$	$8\frac{3}{8}$	$\frac{11}{16}$	125	400	.46	.92
10=NE	11	9	$\frac{3}{4}$	100	400	.60	1.20
12=NE	$12\frac{1}{4}$	$9\frac{1}{2}$	1	80	420	.68	1.36

EXTRA FINISHED IRON HOLLOW WARE

LONG GRIDDLE

No.	Length Inches	Width Inches	Packed in Barrel	Wt. per Bbl. Pounds	Without Bail Plain	Without Bail Nickel Pltd.
7	$16\frac{1}{2}$	$7\frac{1}{4}$	65	410	$ .68	$2.04
8	19	$8\frac{1}{2}$	40	385	.82	2.28
9	21	$9\frac{5}{8}$	30	375	1.04	2.54
10	$24\frac{1}{2}$	$12\frac{1}{2}$	23	420	1.55	3.74
11	25	$13\frac{1}{2}$	18	360	2.20	4.68

With bail add ten cents to list

LONG GRIDDLE

New England

No.	Length Inches	Width Inches	Packed in Barrel	Wt. per Bbl. Pounds	Price List Plain	Price List Nickel Plated
7=NE	$16\frac{3}{8}$	$8\frac{1}{2}$	65	420	$ .68	$2.04
8=NE	$18\frac{3}{4}$	$9\frac{1}{8}$	60	400	.82	2.28
9=NE	$20\frac{1}{2}$	$10\frac{1}{4}$	50	410	1.04	2.54
10=NE	$22\frac{1}{4}$	$11\frac{5}{16}$	40	420	1.55	3.74

EXTRA FINISHED IRON HOLLOW WARE

FLOP GRIDDLE

No. 8, Three Pans...................................per doz., **$13.00**

Each cake, four inches diameter.

GAS OR VAPOR STOVE GRIDDLE

No.	Diameter Inches	Packed in Crate	Wt. per Crate Pounds	Price List
12	12	10	110	**$1.50**

This Polished Iron Griddle is equipped with a hollow base, which prevents the extreme heat of a Gas or Vapor Stove from over-heating the center and distributes the heat evenly under the Griddle.

EXTRA FINISHED IRON HOLLOW WARE

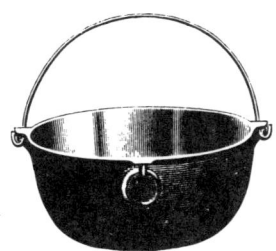

SCOTCH BOWL

No.	Dia. Top Inches	Dia. Bot. Inches	Depth Inches	Capacity Quarts	Packed in Crate	Wt.per Crt. Pounds	Price List Polished	Price List Nick. Pltd.
2	$9\frac{3}{8}$	$4\frac{3}{4}$	$3\frac{3}{4}$	3	25	100	$ .70	$1.40
3	$10\frac{3}{8}$	$5\frac{3}{8}$	$4\frac{1}{8}$	4	25	145	.82	1.64
4	$11\frac{1}{2}$	$6\frac{1}{4}$	$4\frac{3}{8}$	5	20	150	.92	1.84
5	12	$6\frac{3}{4}$	$4\frac{3}{4}$	6	18	150	1.00	2.00

YANKEE BOWL

No.	Dia. Top Inches	Dia. Bot. Inches	Depth Inches	Capacity Quarts	Packed in Crate	Wt.per Crt. Pounds	Price List Polished	Price List Nick. Pltd.
2	$9\frac{1}{2}$	$5\frac{1}{2}$	$5\frac{1}{2}$	4	15	100	$ .88	$1.76
3	$10\frac{3}{8}$	$5\frac{1}{2}$	6	6	15	115	.98	1.96
4	$10\frac{3}{4}$	$5\frac{3}{4}$	$6\frac{1}{2}$	7	15	130	1.10	2.20
5	$11\frac{1}{2}$	$6\frac{3}{4}$	$7\frac{1}{8}$	9	15	145	1.25	2.50

EXTRA FINISHED IRON HOLLOW WARE

DUTCH OVEN—WITH BAIL

No.	Dia. Top Inches	Dia. Bot. Inches	Depth Inches	Capacity Quarts	Pkd. in Crate	Wt. per Crt. Pounds	Price List Polished	Price List Nick. Pltd.
6	8	7	$3\frac{3}{4}$	$2\frac{1}{2}$	25	100	**$1.15**	$2.30
7	9	8	4	$3\frac{1}{2}$	25	120	**1.30**	2.60
8	10	9	$4\frac{1}{4}$	5	25	140	**1.50**	3.00
9	11	$10\frac{1}{4}$	$4\frac{1}{2}$	6	18	130	**1.70**	3.40
10	$12\frac{1}{2}$	11	$5\frac{1}{4}$	8	15	140	**2.00**	4.00
11	$13\frac{1}{4}$	$11\frac{1}{2}$	6	12	12	130	**2.40**	4.80
12	$14\frac{1}{4}$	12	7	14	10	140	**2.90**	5.80
13	$15\frac{1}{4}$	13	8	18	10	150	**3.45**	6.90

Ovens without covers, 30 cents less above lists.
Covers are crated separately.

DUTCH OVEN—BAILED—WITH LEGS
Flange Cover

No.	Dia. Top Inches	Dia. Bot. Inches	Depth Inches	Capacity Quarts	Pkd. in Crate	Wt. per Crate Pounds	Price List Polished
8	10	9	$4\frac{1}{4}$	5	15	95	**$1.65**
9	11	10	$4\frac{1}{2}$	6	15	125	**1.90**
10	$12\frac{1}{2}$	11	$5\frac{1}{4}$	8	10	115	**2.20**
11	$13\frac{1}{4}$	$11\frac{1}{2}$	6	12	10	125	**2.60**
12	$14\frac{1}{4}$	12	7	14	8	130	**3.05**
13	$15\frac{1}{4}$	13	8	18	8	140	**3.60**

Ovens without covers, 40 cents less above lists.
Covers are crated separately.

EXTRA FINISHED IRON HOLLOW WARE

MASLIN SHAPED KETTLE

Size Quarts	Diameter Inches	Depth Inches	Packed in Crate	Wt. per Crate Pounds	Price List Polished	Price List Nick. Pltd
4	9	5	20	120	$ .95	$1.90
6	10	$5\frac{5}{8}$	15	115	1.05	2.10
8	$11\frac{1}{2}$	$6\frac{1}{2}$	15	125	1.30	2.60
12	$12\frac{3}{8}$	$7\frac{1}{2}$	10	125	1.60	3.20

FLAT BOTTOM KETTLE

No.	Dia. Top Inches	Dia. Bot. Inches	Depth Inches	Capacity Quarts	Packed in Crate	Wt. per Crt. Pounds	Price List Polished	Price List Nick. Pltd.
6	$8\frac{1}{4}$	$7\frac{1}{4}$	6	4	6	40	$1.00	$2.00
7	$9\frac{1}{4}$	$8\frac{1}{4}$	$6\frac{1}{4}$	6	6	45	1.10	2.20
8	$9\frac{7}{8}$	$8\frac{7}{8}$	$6\frac{3}{4}$	7	6	55	1.25	2.50
9	$10\frac{3}{4}$	$9\frac{5}{8}$	7	9	6	60	1.55	3.10
10	$11\frac{3}{4}$	$10\frac{5}{8}$	$7\frac{5}{8}$	12	6	70	1.90	3.80

EXTRA FINISHED IRON HOLLOW WARE

LOW KETTLE

No.	Dia. Top Inches	Dia. Bot. Inches	Depth Inches	Capacity Quarts	Pkd. in Crate	Wt. per Crt. Pounds	Price List Polished	Price List Nick. Pltd.
7	$9\frac{1}{4}$	$7\frac{3}{4}$	$6\frac{1}{8}$	5	6	40	**$1.00**	$2.00
8	$9\frac{7}{8}$	$8\frac{1}{2}$	$6\frac{3}{8}$	6	6	45	**1.10**	2.20
9	$10\frac{7}{8}$	$9\frac{1}{2}$	$7\frac{3}{8}$	8	6	50	**1.25**	2.50

REGULAR KETTLE

No.	Dia. Top Inches	Dia. Bot. Inches	Depth Inches	Capacity Quarts	Pkd. in Crate	Wt. per Crt. Pounds	Price List Polished	Price List Nick. Pltd.
6	$8\frac{1}{4}$	$6\frac{5}{8}$	$6\frac{3}{8}$	4	6	40	**$1.00**	$2.00
7	$9\frac{1}{2}$	$7\frac{3}{4}$	$7\frac{1}{4}$	6	6	45	**1.10**	2.20
8	$10\frac{3}{4}$	$8\frac{3}{4}$	8	8	6	55	**1.25**	2.50
9	$11\frac{5}{8}$	$9\frac{3}{4}$	$8\frac{1}{2}$	10	6	70	**1.55**	3.10

EXTRA FINISHED IRON HOLLOW WARE

REGULAR BULGED POT

No.	Dia. Top Inches	Dia. Bot. Inches	Depth Inches	Capacity Quarts	Pkd. in Crate	Wt. per Crt. Pounds	Price List Polished	Price List Nick. Pltd.
6	8¼	6¾	7¾	5	6	45	**$1.30**	$2.60
7	9⅜	7¾	8⅛	7	6	55	**1.40**	2.80
8	10⅜	8¾	8⅝	9	6	70	**1.60**	3.20
9	11½	9¾	9¼	12	6	80	**1.85**	3.70

FLAT BOTTOM BULGED POT

No.	Dia. Top Inches	Dia. Bot. Inches	Depth Inches	Capacity Quarts	Pkd. in Crate	Wt. per Crt. Pounds	Price List Polished	Price List Nick. Pltd.
7	9½	8⅛	7	6	6	55	**$1.40**	$2.80
8	10¼	9	7	8	6	65	**1.60**	3.20
9	11½	10	7⅜	11	6	75	**1.85**	3.70

EXTRA FINISHED IRON HOLLOW WARE

LOW ECCENTRIC KETTLE

No.	Dia. Top Inches	Dia. Pit Inches	Depth Inches	Capacity Quarts	Pkd. in Crate	Wt. per Crt. Pounds	Price List Polished	Price List Nick. Pltd.
7	$9\frac{1}{2}$	$6\frac{1}{8}$	5	4	10	60	**$1.05**	$2.10
8	$10\frac{1}{8}$	$6\frac{7}{8}$	$5\frac{1}{2}$	5	10	70	**1.20**	2.40
9	$11\frac{1}{8}$	8	$5\frac{7}{8}$	7	8	80	**1.45**	2.90

ECCENTRIC KETTLE

No.	Dia. Top Inches	Dia. Pit Inches	Depth Inches	Capacity Quarts	Pkd. in Crate	Wt. per Crt. Pounds	Price List Polished	Price List Nick. Pltd.
7	$10\frac{1}{8}$	6	$7\frac{3}{4}$	7	6	50	**$1.20**	$2.40
8	$10\frac{5}{8}$	$6\frac{3}{4}$	$8\frac{1}{2}$	9	6	60	**1.45**	2.90
9	$11\frac{1}{2}$	8	8	11	6	70	**1.76**	3.52

EXTRA FINISHED IRON HOLLOW WARE

ECCENTRIC BULGED POT

No.	Dia. Top Inches	Dia. Pit Inches	Depth Inches	Capacity Quarts	Pkd. in Crate	Wt. per Crt. Pounds	Price List Polished	Price List Nick. Pltd.
7	$10\frac{5}{8}$	6	$8\frac{5}{8}$	8	6	60	**$1.65**	$3.30
8	$11\frac{3}{4}$	$6\frac{3}{4}$	$9\frac{3}{8}$	12	5	75	**2.00**	4.00
9	$12\frac{1}{8}$	$7\frac{3}{4}$	$10\frac{1}{4}$	15	5	80	**2.50**	5.00

EXTRA LARGE ECCENTRIC POT—Style "B"

No.	Dia. Top Inches	Dia. Pit Inches	Depth Inches	Capacity Quarts	Packed in Crate	Wt. per Crt. Pounds	Price List Polished	Price List Nick. Pltd.
7	$11\frac{7}{8}$	6	10	14	4	70	**$2.50**	$5.00
8	$13\frac{3}{8}$	7	11	20	3	70	**3.25**	6.50
9	$14\frac{1}{2}$	8	$11\frac{3}{4}$	30	3	80	**4.50**	9.00

EXTRA FINISHED IRON HOLLOW WARE

OVAL ROASTER
"Plain Smooth Casting"

Cat. No.	Length Inches	Breadth Inches	Depth Inches	Capacity Quarts	Packed in Crate	Weight per Crate, Lbs.	Price List
3	$12\frac{1}{4}$	$7\frac{3}{8}$	$3\frac{3}{8}$	$3\frac{1}{2}$	20	135	**$1.60**
5	$13\frac{7}{8}$	$9\frac{1}{8}$	$4\frac{1}{4}$	$5\frac{1}{2}$	15	140	**1.95**
7	$15\frac{3}{4}$	$10\frac{3}{4}$	$4\frac{5}{8}$	8	12	150	**2.35**

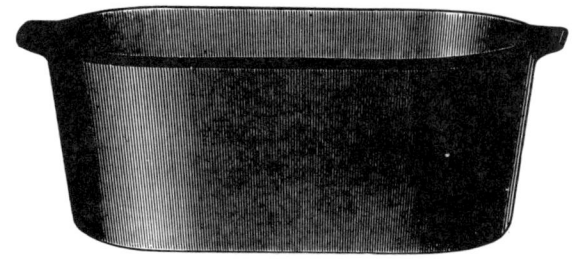

HAM BOILER
"Plain Smooth Casting"
Flat Bottom

Cat. No.	Length Inches	Breadth Inches	Depth Inches	Capacity Gallons	Packed in Crate	Weight per Crate, Lbs.	Price List
8	22	12	$8\frac{1}{2}$	7	8	240	**$2.25**

EXTRA FINISHED IRON HOLLOW WARE

VICTOR SKILLET

No.	Dia. Top Inches	Dia. Bottom Inches	Depth Inches	Packed in Barrel	Wt. per Barrel Pounds	Price List Polished
7V	$9\frac{3}{8}$	8	$1\frac{5}{8}$	100	400	$ .42
8V	10	$8\frac{1}{2}$	$1\frac{3}{4}$	100	410	.46
9V	11	$9\frac{1}{2}$	$1\frac{7}{8}$	85	400	.50

These Skillets are smaller size than the regular Skillet.

TEA KETTLE—PIT OR FLAT BOTTOM

No.	Capacity Quarts	Packed in Crate	Wt. per Crt. Pounds	Plain	Tinned	Nickel Plated Tinned Inside
6	4	5	45	$1.25	$1.65	$3.20
7	5	5	50	1.50	1.90	3.40
8	6	5	55	1.70	2.10	3.60
9	8	5	60	1.90	2.30	4.00

NOTE—We ship *Pit Bottoms* unless flat is specified.

EXTRA FINISHED IRON HOLLOW WARE

COFFEE ROASTER

		List Price Each
No. 3—Cylinder 6 x5½ inches		$1.50
No. 2— " 8 x5½ "		1.75
No. 1— " 9½x7 "		2.00

APPLE CAKE PAN

No. of Cakes	Dia. of Cakes	Depth of Cup	Dia. of Pan	Pkd. in Bbl.	Wt. per Bbl. lbs.	List Price Each
7	2¼	1⅛	9¼"	50	400	$ .70

DANISH CAKE PAN
Same as above without Rim

No. of Cakes	Dia. of Cakes	Depth of Cup	Dia. of Pan	Pkd. in Bbl.	Wt. per Bbl. lbs.	List Price Each
7	2¼	1⅛	9"	50	400	$ .70

PLETT PAN

No. of Cakes	Dia. of Cakes	Depth of Pan	Dia. of Pan	List Price Each
7	3"	¼"	9½"	$ .70

EXTRA FINISHED IRON HOLLOW WARE

GEM PANS

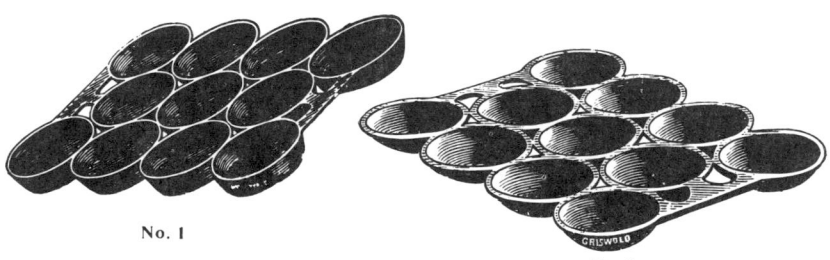

No. 1

No. 3

No.	Size of Pan Inches	Size of Cake Inches	Packed in Barrel Dozens	Wt. per Bbl. Pounds	Price List Per Doz.
1	$11\frac{1}{2}$x$7\frac{3}{4}$	$2\frac{1}{2}$x$\frac{3}{4}$	8	360	**$4.60**
3	$12\frac{1}{2}$x$8\frac{1}{2}$	3 x$\frac{3}{4}$	10	400	**4.60**

No. 5

No. 6

No.	Size of Pan Inches	Size of Cake Inches	Packed in Barrel Dozens	Wt. per Bbl. Pounds	Price List Per Doz.
5	12x$7\frac{1}{2}$	$3\frac{3}{4}$x$2\frac{3}{8}$x$\frac{3}{4}$	11	385	**$4.60**
6	13x$7\frac{1}{2}$	$2\frac{7}{8}$x$1\frac{7}{8}$x$\frac{1}{2}$	12	445	**4.60**

No. 8

No. 9

No.	Size of Pan Inches	Size of Cake Inches	Packed in Barrel Dozens	Wt. per Bbl. Pounds	Price List Per Doz.
8	$12\frac{3}{4}$x$6\frac{3}{4}$	3 x $\frac{7}{8}$	8	380	**$4.60**
9	$10\frac{3}{8}$x7	$2\frac{1}{8}$x1	14	400	**4.60**

EXTRA FINISHED IRON HOLLOW WARE

GEM PANS

No. 10

No. 18

No.	Size of Pan Inches	Size of Cake Inches	Pkd. in Barrel Dozens	Wt. per Barrel Pounds	Price Lsit per Doz.
10	$10\frac{1}{2}$x$7\frac{1}{2}$	$2\frac{1}{2}$x$1\frac{3}{4}$	$7\frac{1}{2}$	510	**$5.80**
18	$8\frac{1}{2}$x5	$2\frac{1}{2}$x$1\frac{3}{4}$	18	490	**2.95**

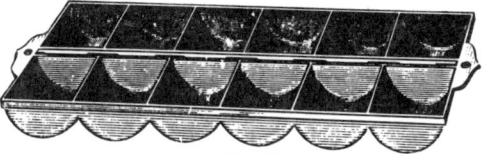

No. 11

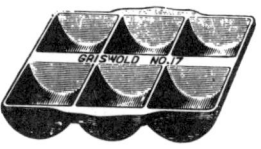

No. 17

No.	Size of Pan Inches	Size of Cake Inches	Packed in Barrel Dozens	Wt. per Bbl. Pounds	Price List per Doz.
11	$11\frac{5}{8}$x$6\frac{7}{8}$	3x$1\frac{7}{8}$x$\frac{7}{8}$	$7\frac{1}{2}$	430	**$4.60**
17	$7\frac{1}{2}$x$5\frac{3}{4}$	3x$1\frac{7}{8}$x$\frac{7}{8}$	16	450	**2.30**

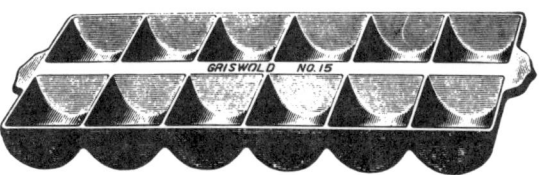

No. 15

No. 16

No.	Size of Pan Inches	Size of Cake Inches	Packed in Barrel Dozens	Wt. per Bbl. Pounds	Price List per Doz.
15	13x8	$3\frac{1}{2}$x2x$1\frac{1}{8}$	6	390	**$7.00**
16	8x$6\frac{1}{2}$	$3\frac{1}{2}$x2x$1\frac{1}{8}$	10	400	**3.50**

EXTRA FINISHED IRON HOLLOW WARE

GEM PANS

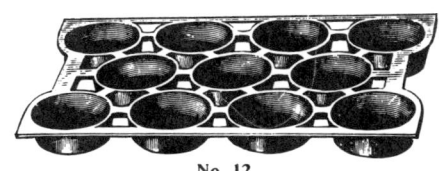

No. 12

No. 20

No.	Size of Pan Inches	Size of Cake Inches	Packed in Barrel Dozens	Wt. per Bbl. Pounds	Price List per Doz.
12	11 x7$\frac{1}{4}$	2$\frac{1}{4}$x$\frac{3}{4}$	10	360	$4.60
20	10$\frac{5}{8}$x7$\frac{1}{2}$	2 x$\frac{3}{4}$	12	390	4.60

No. 19

No.	Size of Pan	Size of Cake	Price List per Doz.
19	6$\frac{1}{2}$"x4$\frac{1}{2}$"	2$\frac{1}{8}$"x1"	$2.30

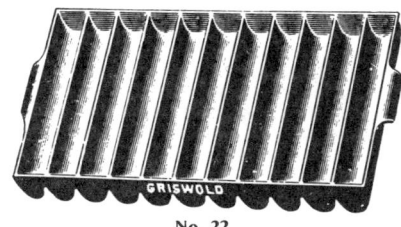

No. 22

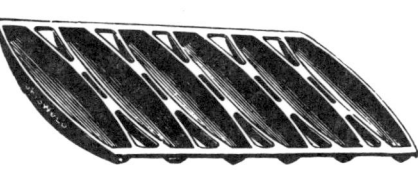

No. 6

BREAD PANS

No.	Size of Pan Inches	Size of Cake Inches	Packed in Barrel Dozens	Wt. per Barrel Pounds	Price List per Doz.
22	13$\frac{3}{8}$x7$\frac{3}{8}$	7x1$\frac{1}{8}$	7	420	$5.80
6	12$\frac{1}{2}$x6$\frac{1}{2}$	6x1$\frac{3}{4}$	12	445	4.60

EXTRA FINISHED IRON HOLLOW WARE

SAD IRON HEATER

	Dia. Top Inches	Dia. Bottom Inches	Packed in Crate	Wt. per Crate Pounds	Price List Each
Round, Polished	10	$10\frac{1}{2}$	24	85	$ .40

SAD IRON HEATER

	Size Top	Size Bottom	Packed in Crate	Wt. per Crate Pounds	Price List Each
Square, Polished	$10\frac{1}{8}''$ sq	$10\frac{7}{8}''$ sq	24	120	$ .50

DEEP LONG PAN, OR IRON HEATER

No.	Lgth. Inside Inches	Width Inside Inches	Packed in Barrel	Wt. per Barrel Pounds	Deep Pat. Plain	Shallow Pat. Plain
7	$15\frac{1}{4}$	$6\frac{1}{2}$	48	315	$ .70	$ .66
8	17	$7\frac{1}{2}$	30	360	.80	.76
9	$19\frac{1}{4}$	$8\frac{1}{4}$	30	390	1.00	.96

WAFFLE IRONS

"AMERICAN"

BULLETIN
NUMBER W-7

THE GRISWOLD MFG. CO.,
ERIE, PENNSYLVANIA, U. S. A.

TERMS.

Sixty days or two per cent discount for cash if paid within 10 days from date of invoice.

All bills payable in New York or other par funds without allowance for exchange.

No charge for crating or cartage.

No freight allowance on shipments weighing less than 200 pounds. Positively no deviation from this rule.

We take special care in the packing of our goods. Every piece carefully packed, insuring against breakage.

After goods are shipped in good order our liability ceases, and we cannot allow any claim for breakage or other damage in transit.

Claims for errors or deficiencies will not be entertained unless made within FIVE DAYS after receipt of goods.

GRISWOLD AMERICAN AND FRENCH PATTERN

WAFFLE IRONS were for many years the only improved Irons made in this or any other country. It was not until the expiration of our patents that any attempt was made to copy our models, and like all copies, they fall far short of the original.

Every piece is made after our own patented design, from the choicest of superior irons, and made by workmen who are skilled in this class of work. Every pan is cast with uniform thickness, even to the outer edge where thickness is necessary to hold the heat for a well baked cake. Ball joints which revolve in the frame at any angle. Grooved rings to catch the overflow. Alaska Cold Wire handles, set in air cooled sockets. Made in many shapes.

Order an assortment. Make a good display, and you will be surprised at the sale of these irons. Write for prices, and try a sample lot.

THE GRISWOLD MFG. COMPANY,
Erie, Pa., U. S. A.

GRISWOLD WAFFLE IRONS

"American" Pattern

Patented

No.	Diameter of Pan. Inches.	Diameter Bottom of Ring. Inches.	Packed in Bbl.	Gross Weight Lbs.	Price List Per Doz.	Price List. Nickel Plated Per Doz.
6	$5\frac{3}{4}$	8	3 doz.	225	$12.00	$21.00
7	$6\frac{3}{4}$	$8\frac{3}{4}$	3 "	260	14.00	24.00
8	$7\frac{3}{4}$	$9\frac{7}{8}$	3 "	360	16.00	27.00
9	$8\frac{5}{8}$	$10\frac{5}{8}$	$2\frac{1}{2}$ "	350	18.00	30.00

Patented

DEEP RING—FOR GAS OR VAPOR STOVES

No.	Diameter of Pan. Inches.	Packed in Bbl.	Gross Weight Lbs.	Price List Per Doz.	Price List. Nickel Plated. Per Doz.
77	$6\frac{3}{4}$	$2\frac{1}{2}$ doz.	320	$17.00	$34.00
88	$7\frac{3}{4}$	2 "	325	19.00	38.00
99	$8\frac{5}{8}$	$1\frac{1}{3}$ "	260	23.00	46.00

GRISWOLD WAFFLE IRONS

"American" Pattern

No. 111

No.	Size of Pan. Inches.	Size of Cake. Inches.	Size of Frame. Inches.	Packed in Bbl.	Gross Weight Lbs.	Price List Per Doz.
111	$6\frac{3}{4}$ x $6\frac{3}{4}$	$3\frac{1}{4}$ x $3\frac{1}{4}$	10 x 10	3 doz.	360	**$18.00**

No. 11

DEEP RING—FOR GAS OR VAPOR STOVES

No.	Size of Pan. Inches.	Size of Cake. Inches.	Size of Frame. Inches.	Packed in Bbl.	Gross Weight Lbs.	Price List. Per Doz.
11	$6\frac{3}{4}$x$6\frac{3}{4}$	$3\frac{1}{4}$x$3\frac{1}{4}$	10x10	2 doz.	325	**$19.00**

GRISWOLD WAFFLE IRONS

"American" Pattern

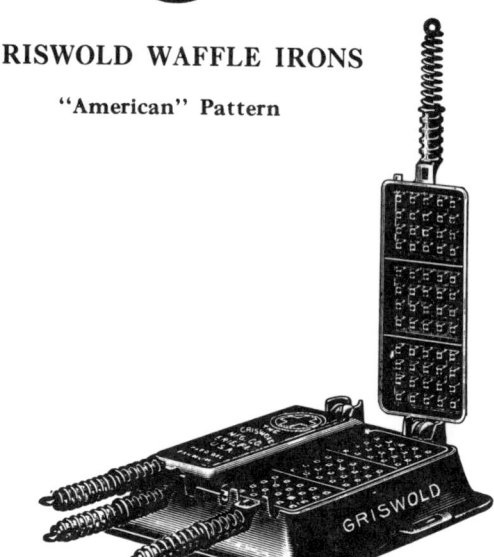

No. 12—Patented

No.	Size of Pan. Inches.	Size of Cake. Inches.	Size of Frame. Inches.	Packed in Bbl.	Gross Weight Lbs.	Price List. Per Doz.
12	9½ x 4	3 x 4	11 x 12	1½ doz.	300	**$33.00**

No. 13—Patented

No.	Size of Pan. Inches.	Size of Cake. Inches.	Size of Frame. Inches.	Packed in Bbl.	Gross Weight Lbs.	Price List. Per Doz.
13	9½ x 4	3 x 4	15 x 12	1 doz.	290	**$49.50**

GRISWOLD WAFFLE IRONS
"American" Pattern

No. 14.—Patented.

No.	Size of Pan. Inches.	Size of Cake. Inches.	Size of Frame. Inches.	Packed in Bbl.	Gross Weight Lbs.	Price List. Per Doz.
14	$9\frac{1}{2}$ x 4	3 x 4	19 x 12	$\frac{3}{4}$ doz.	280	**$66.00**

"French" Pattern

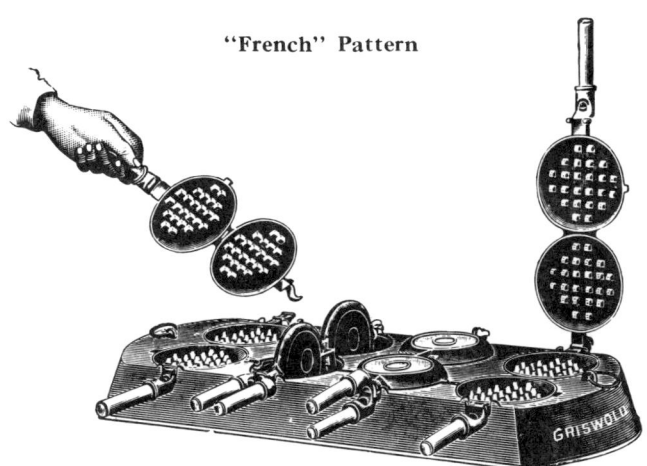

Patented.

No.	Pair of Pans.	Diameter of Pan. Inches.	Length of Frame. Inches.	Width of Frame. Inches.	Packed in Bbl.	Gross Weight Lbs.	Price List. Per Doz.
7	2	4	$14\frac{1}{2}$	$11\frac{1}{2}$	1 doz.	200	**$33.00**
8	3	4	20	$11\frac{1}{2}$	1 "	275	**49.50**
9	4	4	$22\frac{1}{2}$	$11\frac{1}{2}$	$\frac{1}{2}$ "	190	**66.00**

GRISWOLD WAFFLE IRONS

SQUARE WAFFLE IRON

No.	No. of Cakes.	Size of Cake. Inches.	Length of Pan. Inches.	Width of Pan. Inches.	Price List. Per Doz.
2	3	$4\frac{1}{2}$ x $2\frac{3}{8}$	$7\frac{1}{2}$	$4\frac{3}{4}$	$22.00
1	3	$4\frac{7}{8}$ x $2\frac{3}{4}$	$8\frac{3}{4}$	5	26.00
0	4	$4\frac{3}{4}$ x $2\frac{3}{4}$	$9\frac{3}{4}$	6	32.00
00	6	$4\frac{7}{8}$ x $2\frac{3}{8}$	10	$7\frac{3}{4}$	36.00

OVAL WAFFLE IRON

No.	Length of Pan. Inches.	Width of Pan. Inches.	Size of Cake. Inches.	Fits Stove No.	Price List. Per Doz.
7	$17\frac{3}{4}$	$7\frac{1}{2}$	$4\frac{7}{8}$ x $2\frac{3}{8}$	7	$36.00
8	$19\frac{1}{2}$	$8\frac{5}{8}$	5 x $2\frac{5}{8}$	8	46.00
9	21	$9\frac{1}{2}$	$5\frac{1}{2}$ x $2\frac{3}{4}$	9	52.00

GRISWOLD WAFER IRON

No.	Diameter of Pan. Inches.	Diameter of Ring. Inches.	Packed in Box.	Gross Weight Lbs.	Price List Per Doz.
1.	$5\frac{3}{8}$	$8\frac{1}{2}$	1 doz.	50	**$16.00**

"American" Pattern

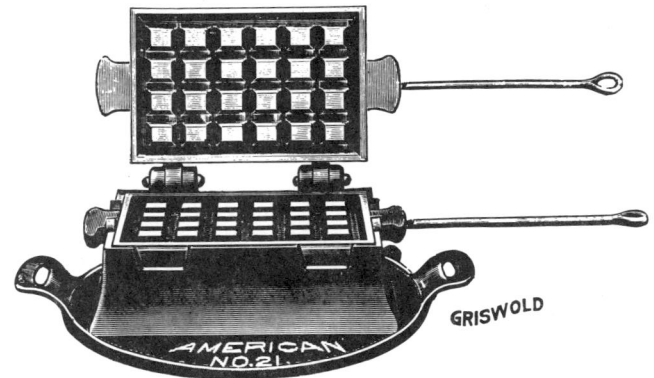

No.	Size of Pan. Inches.	Packed in Bbl.	Gross Weight Lbs.	Price List. Per Doz.
21.	$4 \times 6\frac{1}{2}$	2 doz.	350	**$32.00**

This pattern of American Waffle Iron is made with exceptionally heavy cast iron pans; this additional weight provides for the holding of the heat for a longer time, and adds very much to the delicacy of the flavor of the waffle cake.

GRISWOLD STOVE AND WAFFLE IRON

	Packed in Crate.	Weight Crated. Pounds.	Price List.
No. 130, Gas Stove and			
No. 13, Waffle Iron (with three pans)...................1		45	**$11.75**
No. 140, Gas Stove and			
No. 14, Waffle Iron (with four pans).....................1		56	**15.00**

The stove frame is of heavy steel, nickeled feet and trimmings, and has separate burner under each pan.

GRISWOLD STOVE AND GRIDDLE

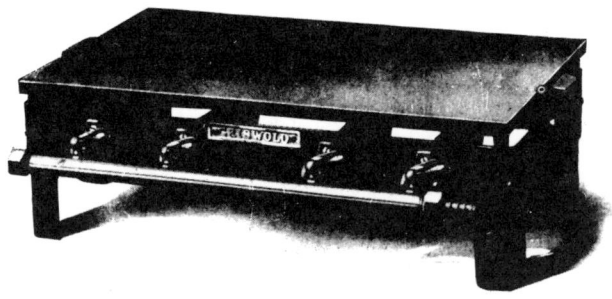

	Packed in Crate.	Weight Crated. Pounds.	Price List.
No. 130, Gas Stove and			
No. 135, Griddle (18 x 13½ inches)..........................1		43	**$11.00**
No. 140, Gas Stove and			
No. 145, Griddle (22 x 13½ inches)..........................1		54	**14.00**

These Griddles are extra heavy and highly polished. The No. 130 stove has three burners and the No. 140 stove has four burners.

Also sold in sets of one Stove. Waffle and Griddle.

No.	Price List. Each.	No.	Price List. Each.
13 Waffle Iron only............**$4.15**		**14** Waffle Iron only............**$5.50**	
130 Stove only................. **7.60**		**140** Stove only................. **9.50**	
135 Griddle only............... **3.40**		**145** Griddle only............... **4.50**	

In Ordering, specify for Natural or Artificial Gas.

PATTY IRONS

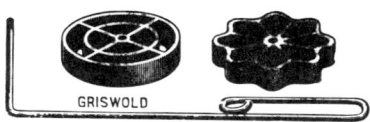

Set No. 1

Price List.

No. 1, Shallow Style. . . . . .per doz. set **$7.00**

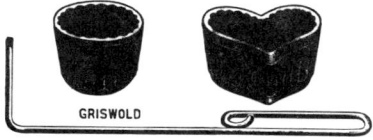

Set No. 2

Price List.

No. 2, Deep Style. . . . . .per doz. set **$7.00**

Each set of two irons and wire handle packed in neat display box.

Dampers
and
Stove Hardware

"AMERICAN"

BULLETIN
Number D-5

THE GRISWOLD MFG. CO.
ERIE, PENNSYLVANIA, U. S. A.

"AMERICAN" DAMPER

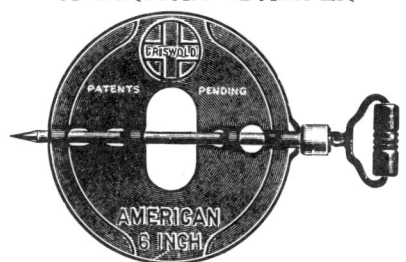

Steel Spindle
Enameled Wood Handle. Nickel Steel Ferrule

		Packed in Bbls.	Gross Wt. Bbls.	Price List. Per Doz.
3	inch	120 doz	380 lbs	**$1.15**
4	"	60 "	320 "	**1.25**
4½	"	60 "	335 "	**1.30**
5	"	50 "	325 "	**1.35**
5½	"	50 "	400 "	**1.45**
5¾	"	50 "	450 "	**1.50**
6	"	50 "	450 "	**1.50**
6½	"	48 "	465 "	**1.75**
7	"	36 "	480 "	**2.50**

Steel Spindle
Nickel Handle and Ferrule

		Packed in Bbls.	Gross Wt. Bbls.	Price List Per Doz.
3	inch	120 doz	380 lbs	**$1.15**
4	"	60 "	320 "	**1.25**
4½	"	60 "	335 "	**1.30**
5	"	50 "	325 "	**1.35**
5½	"	50 "	400 "	**1.45**
5¾	"	50 "	450 "	**1.50**
6	"	50 "	450 "	**1.50**
6½	"	48 "	465 "	**1.75**
7	"	36 "	480 "	**2.50**

All sizes with either handle made with solid plates for hot air pipes. We always ship open plates unless solid are specified.

"AMERICAN" DAMPER

Steel Spindle
Nickel Coil or Wood Handle
Oval Pattern

			Packed in Bbls.	Gross Wt. Bbls.	Price List Per Doz.
4 inch—Plate	$4\frac{3}{4}$x2	in	60 doz	450 lbs	$1.55
$5\frac{1}{2}$ " "	$6\frac{3}{8}$x$3\frac{1}{4}$	"	60 "	485 "	1.75
6 " "	$6\frac{7}{8}$x$3\frac{3}{4}$	"	60 "	500 "	2.00
7 " "	$7\frac{7}{8}$x$3\frac{3}{4}$	"	50 "	500 "	2.50
8 " "	$8\frac{3}{4}$x$3\frac{3}{4}$	"	40 "	540 "	3.00

Steel Spindle
Furnace Sizes.   Nickel Coil or Wood Handle
No. 14, 15, 16 in. have Cast Spindle.

	Packed in Bbls.	Gross Wt. Bbls.	Price List Per Doz.
8 inch	28 doz	480 lbs	$ 4.00
9 "	20 "	500 "	5.00
10 "	16 "	525 "	6.00
12 "	10 "	450 "	7.00
14 "	5 "	350 "	11.00
15 "	4 "	375 "	13.00
16 "	4 "	410 "	15.00

These large sizes are furnished with solid plates when ordered.
We always ship open plates unless solid are specified.

"AMERICAN" DAMPER CLIP

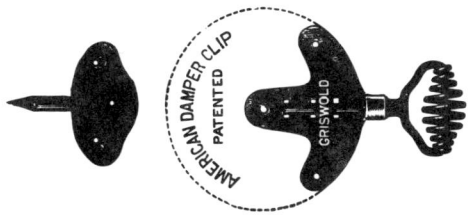

Clip No. 1

Nickel Coil Handle

Size of Plate, 3 in. long, $3\frac{3}{8}$ in. wide.

	Packed in Bbls.	Gross Weight Bbls.		
No. 1 (clips only)	120 doz	380 lbs	per doz.	**$1.25**
" 1, with tail piece			"	**1.35**

Clip No. 2

Nickel Coil Handle

Size of Plate, 5 in. long, $4\frac{3}{4}$ in. wide.

	Packed in Bbls.	Gross Weight Bbls.		
No. 2 (clips only)	60 doz	400 lbs	per doz.	**$1.40**
" 2, with tail piece			"	**1.50**

HOUSEHOLD
HARDWARE
SPECIALTIES

BULLETIN
NUMBER K-4

THE GRISWOLD MFG. CO.
ERIE, PENNSYLVANIA, U. S. A.

S-5-66

FOOD CHOPPER.

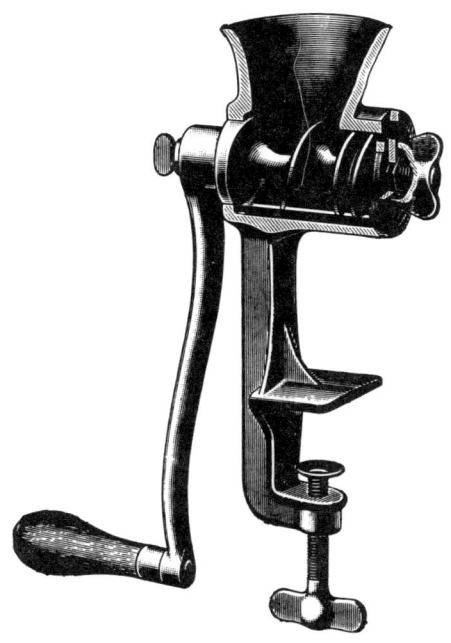

This cut shows the internal shear cut produced by the exact fit of the scroll to the *Straight Knife Edged Rib*, which begins the cutting process the moment the food enters the hopper. The ribs on inside of cutter are straight and each one is machined to a sharp edge which comes in contact with scroll, thus causing the contents to be partly cut in pieces before passing through the knives. *Straight Ribbed* Cutter will discharge more actually cut food per minute than cutters with spiral ribs, where the contents of the cutter follows the spiral rib several times around the inside of body before passing out through the knives. We would call special attention to the size of the hoppers on all sizes which are larger than those on any other cutter, giving them larger capacity. All parts made strictly interchangeable. Nice, smooth castings, well tinned.

Each Chopper equipped with four Cutters. These Cutters are made of special steel, milled true on both sides, giving a perfect cutting surface, superior to a ground knife. The Cutters are easily taken off. Cannot be put on wrong. Making the Griswold "Erie" the simplest and most perfect Chopper on the market.

FOOD CHOPPER.

No. 10

No. 10 . . . . Per Doz. **$10.80**

Weight, $3\frac{1}{2}$ lbs.   Capacity, $1\frac{3}{4}$ lbs. of meat per minute.   Diameter of hopper, $2\frac{1}{8}$x$3\frac{1}{4}$ inches.   Diameter of barrel $2\frac{1}{4}$ inches.   Furnished with four milled double-edge steel cutters—coarse, medium, fine and nut butter.

Packed one in a box, six in a case.   Weight per case, 28 lbs.

FOOD CHOPPER.

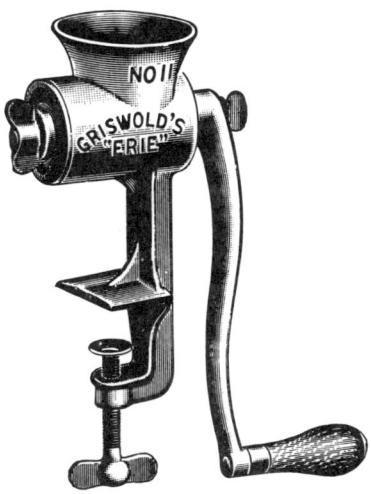

No. 11

No. 11 . . . . Per Doz. **$15.00**

Weight, $4\frac{1}{4}$ lbs. Capacity, $2\frac{1}{4}$ lbs. of meat per minute. Diameter of hopper, $3 \times 3\frac{7}{8}$ inches. Diameter of barrel $2\frac{1}{4}$ inches. Furnished with four milled double-edge steel cutters—coarse, medium, fine and nut butter.

Packed one in a box, six in a case. Weight per case, 32 lbs.

FOOD CHOPPER.

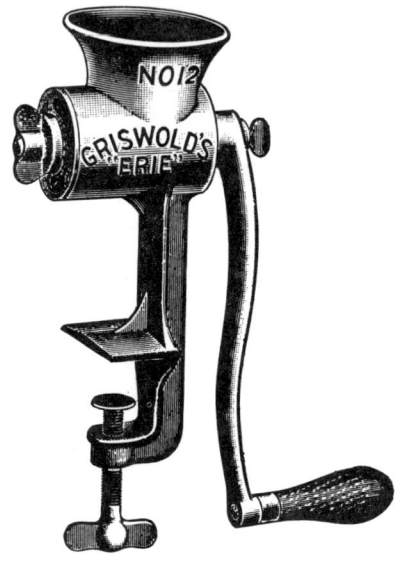

No. 12

No. 12. . . . . Per Doz. **$18.00**

Weight, $4\frac{3}{4}$ lbs. Capacity, $2\frac{1}{2}$ lbs. of meat per minute. Diameter of hopper, $3\frac{3}{8}$x$4\frac{3}{8}$ inches. Diameter of barrel $2\frac{1}{4}$ inches. Furnished with four milled double-edge steel cutters—coarse, medium, fine and nut butter.

Packed one in a box, six in a case. Weight per case, 35 lbs.

FOOD CHOPPER.

No. 13

No. 13 . . . . Per Doz. **$24.00**

Weight, 7 lbs. Capacity, $3\frac{1}{2}$ lbs. of meat per minute. Diameter of hopper, 5x$4\frac{1}{4}$ inches. Diameter of barrel $2\frac{1}{2}$ inches. Furnished with four milled double-edge steel cutters —coarse, medium, fine and extra fine.

The No. 13 is an extra large, strong chopper for use in hotels and restaurants.

Packed one in a box, six in a case. Weight per case, 66 lbs.

PRICE LIST OF REPAIRS FOR THE "GRISWOLD" FOOD CHOPPERS.

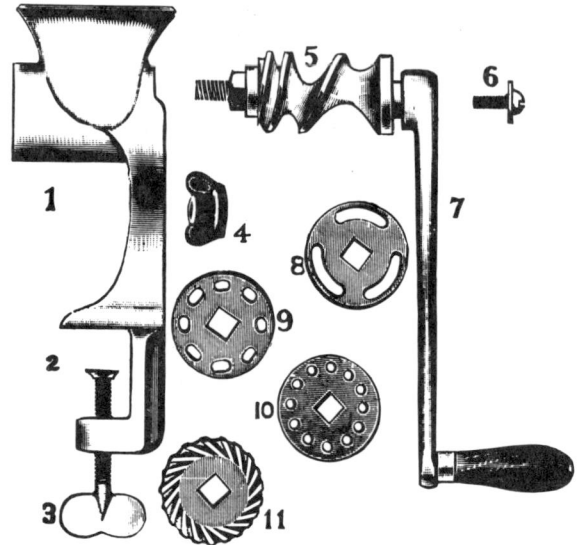

Number of Part	Name of Part	For Chopper			
		No. 10	No. 11	No. 12	No. 13
Fig. 1—Body		**$0.50**	**$0.60**	**$0.75**	**$1.25**
" 2—Table Clamp Plate		.05	.10	.10	.15
" 3—Table Clamp Screw		.15	.15	.15	.20
" 4—Feed Scroll Thumb Nut		.10	.10	.10	.10
" 5—Feed Scroll		.30	.40	.50	.75
" 6—Crank Screw and Washer		.05	.05	.05	.05
" 7—Crank		.20	.25	.25	.30
" 8—Coarse Cutter, $\frac{5}{16}$x$1\frac{9}{32}$ opening		.15	.15	.15	.20
" 9—Medium Cutter, $\frac{5}{16}$x$\frac{5}{8}$ "		.15	.15	.15	.20
" 10—Fine Cutter, $\frac{5}{16}$ opening		.15	.15	.15	.20
" 11—Nut Butter Cutter		.15	.15	.15	.20

COMBINATION MEAT AND FOOD CUTTER embodying all the latest improvements of both Meat Cutter and Food Chopper, making the best and most practical household cutter ever offered to the trade.

Open faced, it discharges freely and cleans easily. The body is funnel shaped, with the scroll passing in from the face. With large opening at face, and small opening at the back, making impossible the escape of juices to drip on floor.

Four bladed steel knife operated against the inside of slightly concaved steel plate, which are drawn tightly together by a three point bearing cam ring. Cutting evenly at all times. Knives and plates are larger than barrel of cutter, giving greater capacity with less resistance.

Knives made from special steel are reversible and self-sharpening. All cast parts doubly coated with pure block tin.

Write for prices and sample lot.

THE GRISWOLD MFG. COMPANY,

Erie, Penna., U. S. A.

COMBINATION MEAT AND FOOD CUTTER.

No. 110

No. 110 . . . . Per Doz. **$12.50**

Small family size. Capacity, $2\frac{1}{2}$ lbs. of meat per minute. Height from table $5\frac{1}{4}$ inches. Diameter of hopper $2\frac{1}{2}$x$3\frac{1}{4}$ inches. Length of barrel $3\frac{13}{32}$ inches. Crank $6\frac{3}{8}$ inches. Weight 3 lbs. 10 oz.

Packed one in a box, six in a case. Weight per case, 30 lbs.

COMBINATION MEAT AND FOOD CUTTER.

No. 111

No. 111 . . . . Per Doz. **$17.00**

Regular family size.   Capacity, 3 lbs. of meat per minute.   Height from table 6 inches.   Diameter of hopper $2\frac{3}{4}$x$3\frac{3}{4}$ inches.   Length of barrel $3\frac{9}{64}$ inches.   Crank $7\frac{1}{2}$ inches.   Weight 4 lbs. 7 oz.

Packed one in a box, six in a case.   Weight per case, 37 lbs.

COMBINATION MEAT AND FOOD CUTTER.

No. 112

No. 112 . . . . Per Doz. **$20.00**

Large family size. Capacity, $3\frac{1}{2}$ lbs. of meat per minute. Height from table $6\frac{1}{2}$ inches. Diameter of hopper $3\frac{1}{8}$x$4\frac{1}{4}$ inches. Length of barrel $3\frac{9}{64}$ inches. Crank $7\frac{1}{2}$ inches. Weight 4 lbs. 9 oz.

Packed one in a box, six in a case. Weight per case, 40 lbs.

COMBINATION MEAT AND FOOD CUTTER.

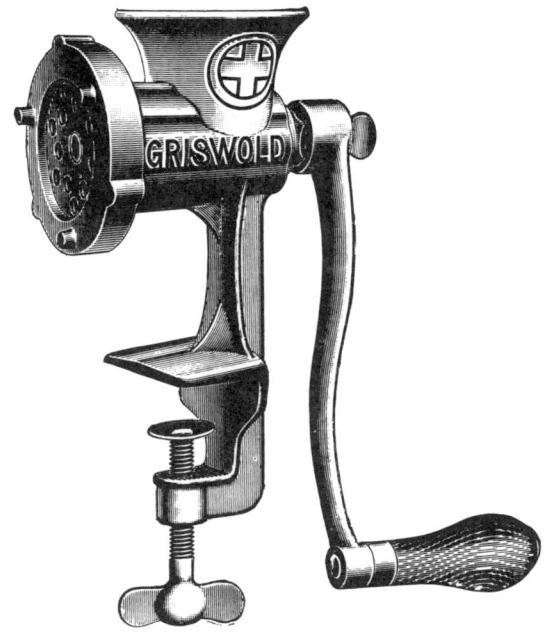

No. 113

No. 113 . . . . Per Doz. **$28.00**

Hotel or Restaurant size. Capacity, 4 lbs. of meat per minute. Height from table $7\frac{1}{4}$ inches. Diameter of hopper $3\frac{7}{8}$x$4\frac{7}{8}$ inches. Length of barrel $4\frac{1}{3}\frac{5}{2}$ inches. Crank $9\frac{3}{8}$ inches. Weight 6 lbs. 9 oz.

Packed one in a box, six in a case. Weight per case, 60 lbs.

COMBINATION MEAT AND FOOD CUTTER.

Hotel, Restaurant or Meat Market sizes. Quickly attached or detached. Can be placed in refrigerator when not in use.

No. 122 . . Per Doz. **$20.00**

No. 122

Size of No. 122 compares with No. 112 and No. 123 with No. 113.

Packed one in a box and six in a case. Weight per case:

No. 122. . . . . . .37 lbs.
No. 123. . . . . . .70 lbs.

No. 123 . . Per Doz. **$28.00**

No. 123

STUFFER ATTACHMENT TO FIT CUTTERS Nos. 110, 111, 112, 113, 122, 123.

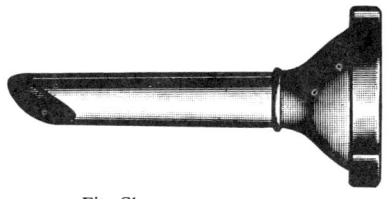

No.	Fits Chopper Numbers		
1	110	Per Doz.	**$4.50**
2	111-112-122	" "	**5.00**
3	113-123	" "	**5.50**

Made of cast iron, heavily coated with pure block tin.
Packed one in a box.   Weight per doz., 15 lbs.

REPAIR PARTS FOR COMBINATION MEAT AND FOOD CUTTERS.

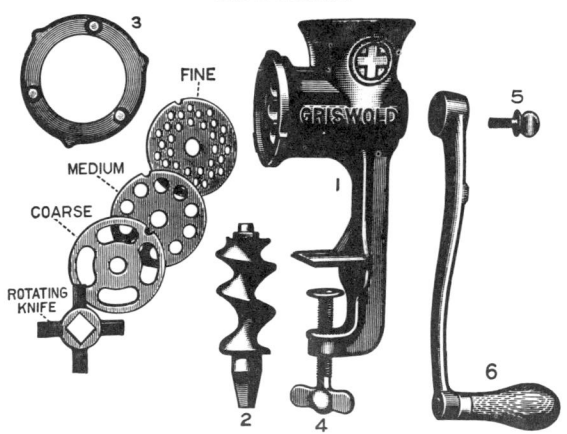

Name	Cut Number		For Cutter Number		
		110	111	112	113
Body	1	$0.50	$0.60	$0.70	$1.05
Scroll	2	.30	.40	.50	.70
Cam Ring	3	.10	.15	.30	.40
Clamp Screw	4	.05	.05	.05	.10
Adj. Screw	5	.10	.10	.10	.10
Crank	6	.20	.20	.25	.25
Fine Knife		.15	.15	.15	.15
Medium Knife		.15	.15	.15	.15
Coarse Knife		.15	.15	.15	.15
Rotating Knife		.15	.15	.15	.15

Repairs for Choppers 122 and 123 are same as 112 and 113 with 15 cents extra for dove-tail bench plate when ordering body.

FRUIT AND LARD PRESS.

Cast Iron Cylinder.   Retinned.

Cat. No.	Capacity Quarts.		Net Weight Each.	List Price. Each.
20 . . . . 4 . . . . Packed 1 in crate . . . . . . 20 lbs **$5.00**				

FRUIT AND LARD PRESS.

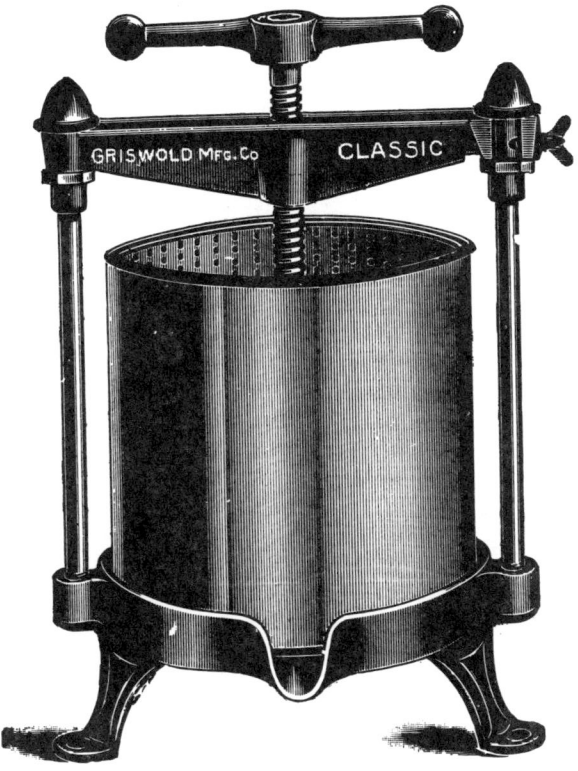

All Parts finished in Bright Tin.

No.	Capacity Quarts.	Net Weight Each.	List Price, Each.
1	2	8½ lbs	2.50 ~~$2.00~~
2	4	19½ "	4.00
3	10	36 "	6.00

This press is very heavy and strong. All parts subject to strain are made of steel. The cylinders are of heavy tin, and all parts have a heavy coating of pure block tin.

CAST POST BOXES.

No. 3

6 inches wide, 12 inches long, 3 inches deep.

No.   3—Japanned and Gold......................Per Doz. **$15.00**
"   30—Antique Bronze.......................... "   "   **20.00**

No. 4

6 inches wide, 12 inches long, $2\frac{3}{4}$ inches deep.

No. 4—Japanned and Gold.......................Per Doz. **$12.00**

TOBACCO CUTTERS.

No. 1—ERIE.

Opening $4\frac{1}{2}$ inches wide, $1\frac{1}{2}$ inches high.

No. 1—Japanned, Gold Striped...................... Per Doz. **$24.00**

Packed one dozen in a case.   Weight per case, 85 lbs.

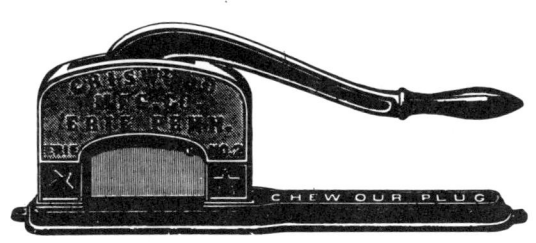

No. 2—ERIE.

Opening $4\frac{1}{2}$ inches wide, $1\frac{3}{8}$ inches high.

No.   2—Japanned................................. Per Doz. **$26.00**
"   **20**—Japanned, with Nickel Base and Handle......   "   "   **35.00**
"   **25**—Full Nickel...............................   "   "   **40.00**

Packed one dozen in a case.   Weight per case, 130 lbs.

The above cutters are fitted with nickel plated name plate, on which we cast a customer's name or advertisement, when ordered in six dozen lots, free of charge.

TOBACCO CUTTERS.

No. 3—TRIUMPH PATTERN.

Opening $4\frac{1}{2}$ inches wide, $1\frac{5}{8}$ inches high.

No. 3—Japanned, Gold Striped.....................Per Doz. **$25.00**

Packed one-half dozen in a case.   Weight per case, 60 lbs.

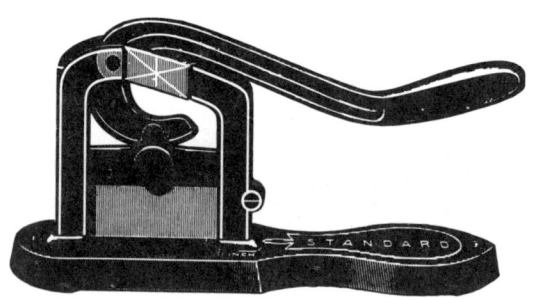

No. 4—STANDARD PATTERN.

Opening $3\frac{5}{8}$ inches wide, $1\frac{1}{2}$ inches high.

No. 4—Japanned, Gold Striped.....................Per Doz. **$19.00**

Packed one-half dozen in a case.   Weight per case, 42 lbs.

Our Tobacco Cutters are extra strong, finely finished, tempered steel knives, and guaranteed perfect in every way.

We also pack them one in a box, or any way required, at slight extra charge.

GAS
HOT PLATES

BULLETIN
NUMBER R-8

THE GRISWOLD MFG. CO.,
ERIE, PENNSYLVANIA, U. S. A.

HOT PLATES

ARE MADE in twenty-four distinct series, embodying many valuable improvements not found in other Plates. All the better Plates are equipped with detachable Drilled or Sawed one-piece Burners. The Cheaper Plates are made with loose Cap Burners. (See pages No. 20 to 23 inc.)

All Hot Plates are furnished with Needle or Lever Valves and Adjustable Air Mixers, except on the No. 500 and No. 1000 Series. Our regular Stock Plates are made with Lever Valves, Corner Legs on the two burner plates, Truss Legs on the three burner plates, except No. 1003, which has corner legs. No. 800 Series is equipped with Removable Dirt Pan, and is always furnished with corner legs (same as illustrated). Special Name Plates furnished when desired if sufficient quantity is ordered. Equipped for either Natural or Artificial Gas.

In using manufactured gas, if the gas pops back and ignites in the air mixer, it indicates too much air for the amount of gas. To remedy, either slightly close Mixer, or increase gas supply, by opening Adjusting Needle. In extreme cases where the gas pressure is very low, it will be necessary to substitute a larger size orifice tip.

In ordering, mention Bulletin R-8.

Specify the City Gas pressure if possible. Always give the number of Plate, style of Burner, Needle or Lever Valves, Natural or Artificial Gas.

Unless otherwise specified we will ship Corner Legs on two Burner, Truss Legs on three Burner Plates (except on No. 803 and No. 1003). We will also ship all Plates with Lever Valves unless otherwise ordered. Weights given are as near correct as possible owing to variation in weight of casting material.

In ordering repairs refer to casting number.

GRISWOLD HOT PLATES are unquestionably the best, and are the most modern and complete line ever offered. Satisfaction positively guaranteed.

THE GRISWOLD MFG. COMPANY,

Erie, Pennsylvania, U. S. A.

SERIES No. 100

An Extra Large Heavy Plate   **Flush Grate Tops**

Needle or Lever Valves

Furnished with Dirt Pans

Size of Top, 25 x 15 inches. Height, 5½ inches. Weight crated, 50 pounds.
One 4½-inch Single and One 6½-inch Double Burners

	Drilled or Sawed Burner
No. 102, Plain	$ 6.00
No. 102, Full Nickel	7.50

Size of Top, 35 x 15 inches. Height, 6 inches. Weight crated, 60 pounds.
Two 4½-inch Single and One 6½-inch Double Burners

	Drilled or Sawed Burner
No. 103, Plain	$ 8.50
No. 103, Full Nickel	10.50

In ordering, specify for Natural or Artificial Gas.

SERIES No. 200

Flush Grate Tops   **Center Draft Burners**   **Needle or Lever Valves**

Size of Top, 12 x 12 inches.   Height, 6 inches.   Weight crated, 15 pounds.
One Single 4½-inch Burner

	Drilled or Sawed Burner
No. 201, Plain..	**$ 2.40**
No. 201, Full Nickel...	**3.15**

Size of Top, 25 x 12 inches.   Height, 6 inches.   Weight crated, 32 pounds.
Two Single 4½-inch Burners

	Drilled or Sawed Burner
No. 202, Plain..	**$4.25**
No. 202, Full Nickel...	**5.25**

Size of Top, 35 x 12 inches.   Height, 6 inches.   Weight crated, 45 pounds.
Three Single 4½-inch Burners

	Drilled or Sawed Burner
No. 203, Plain..	**$ 6.35**
No. 203, Full Nickel...	**7.60**

In ordering, specify for Natural or Artificial Gas.

SERIES No. 200

Flush Grate Tops   **Center Draft Burners**   **Needle or Lever Valves**

Size of Top, 25 x 22 inches.   Height, 6 inches.   Weight crated, 46 pounds.

Three Single 4½-inch Burners

	Drilled or Sawed Burner
No. 204, Plain	$ 7.35
No. 204, Full Nickel	9.35

Size of Top, 25 x 22 inches.   Height, 6 inches.   Weight crated, 50 pounds.

Four Single 4½-inch Burners

	Drilled or Sawed Burner
No. 205, Plain	$ 8.75
No. 205, Full Nickel	10.75

CENTER DRAFT BURNERS used on our No. 200 Series are a most important improvement. On the under side of the stove top is a deep flange or bowl surrounding the burner and projecting below it. This gives a FORCED DRAFT to the burner and greatly increases its heating power. It also prevents the heat striking down onto table or whatever the stove rests on, or the wind from blowing the flame to one side. On this FORCED DRAFT RING, patent has recently been sustained by a decree of the U. S. Circuit Court.

In ordering, specify for Natural or Artificial Gas.

SERIES No. 300

Steel Frame — **Needle or Lever Valves** — **Flush Grate Tops**

Size of Top, 11 x 11 inches.   Height, 6 inches.   Weight crated, 12 pounds.   Drilled or Sawed Burner

One Single 4½-inch Burner

	Drilled or Sawed Burner
No. 301, Plain, Japanned Frame..	**$ 2.05**
No. 301, Full Polished Nickel...	**2.80**

Size of Top, 22 x 11 inches.   Height, 6 inches.   Weight crated, 25 pounds.   Drilled or Sawed Burner

Two Single 4½-inch Burners

	Drilled or Sawed Burner
No. 302, Plain, Japanned Frame..	**$ 3.75**
No. 302, Full Polished Nickel...	**4.50**

Size of Top, 33 x 11 inches.   Height, 6 inches.   Weight crated, 30 pounds.   Drilled or Sawed Burner

Three Single 4½-inch Burners

	Drilled or Sawed Burner
No. 303, Plain, Japanned Frame..	**$ 5.10**
No. 303, Full Polished Nickel...	**6.10**

In ordering, specify for Natural or Artificial Gas.

SERIES No. 500

Flush Grate Tops   **Slip Connection on No. 501**

Needle or Lever Valves on Nos. 502 and 503

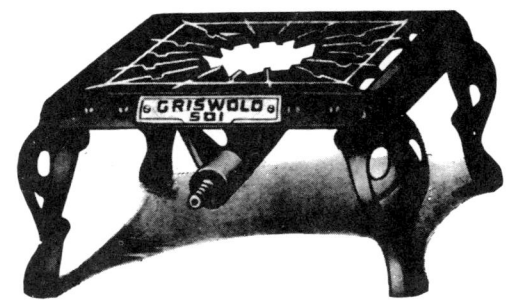

Size of Top, 10½ x 10½ inches. Height, 5½ inches. Weight crated, 10 pounds.
One Single 3½-inch Burner

	Loose Cap Burner	Drilled or Sawed Burner
No. 501, Japanned	$ 1.50	$ 1.60
No. 501, Full Nickel	2.00	2.10

Size of Top, 10½ x 20 inches. Height, 5½ inches. Weight crated, 18 pounds.
Two Single 3½-inch Burners

	Loose Cap Burner	Drilled or Sawed Burner
No. 502, Japanned	$ 2.50	$ 2.65
No. 502, Full Nickel	3.25	3.40

Size of Top, 10½ x 30 inches. Height, 5½ inches. Weight crated, 28 pounds.
Three Single 3½-inch Burners

	Loose Cap Burner	Drilled or Sawed Burner
No. 503, Japanned	$ 3.75	$ 4.00
No. 503, Full Nickel	4.75	5.00

NOTE—We always ship these plates with cast burners unless others are ordered.
In ordering, specify for Natural or Artificial Gas.

SERIES No. 600

Flush Grate Tops

Needle or Lever Valves

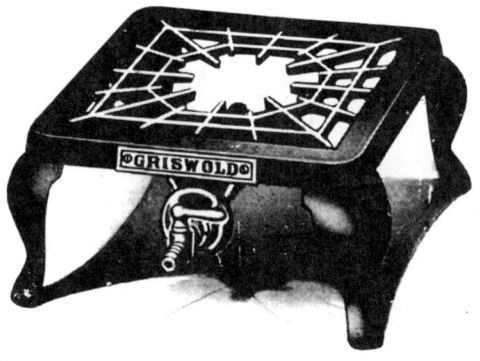

Size of Top, 10 x 10 inches.   Height, 5 inches.   Weight crated, 10 pounds.
One Single 3½-inch Burner

		Drilled or Sawed Burner
No. 601, Plain		$ 1.65
No. 601, Full Nickel		2.15

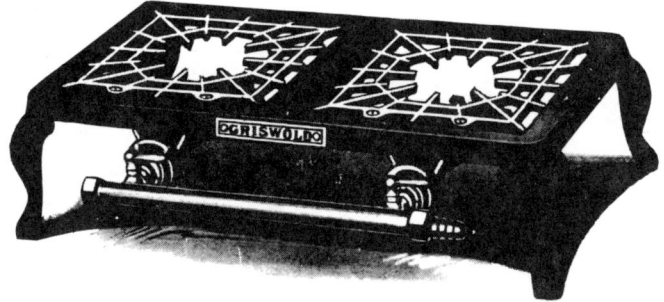

Size of Top, 10 x 20 inches.   Height, 5 inches.   Weight crated, 18 pounds.
Two Single 3½-inch Burners

		Drilled or Sawed Burner
No. 602, Plain		$ 2.75
No. 602, Full Nickel		3.50

Size of Top, 10 x 30 inches.   Height, 5 inches.   Weight crated, 28 pounds.
Three Single 3½-inch Burners

		Drilled or Sawed Burner
No. 603, Plain		$ 4.15
No. 603, Full Nickel		5.15

In ordering, specify for Natural or Artificial Gas.

SERIES No. 700-B

Reversible Grates, Raised or Flush   **Needle or Lever Valves**

Size of Top, 11¾ x 11¾ inches. Height, 6 inches. Weight crated, 13 pounds.

One Single 4½-inch Burner

	Drilled or Sawed Burner
No. 701-B, Plain	$ 1.85
No. 701-B, Full Nickel	2.60

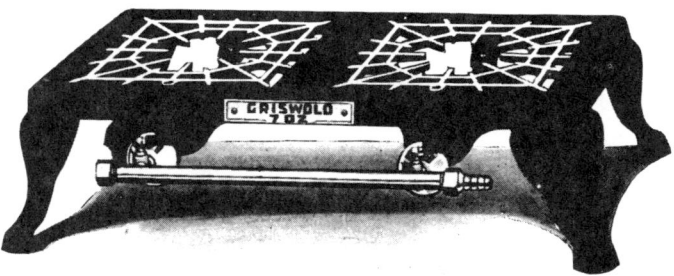

Size of Top, 23 x 11¾ inches. Height, 6 inches. Weight crated, 25 pounds.

Two Single 4½-inch Burners

	Drilled or Sawed Burner
No. 702-B, Plain	$ 3.70
No. 702-B, Full Nickel	4.70

Size of Top, 33 x 11¾ inches. Height, 6 inches. Weight crated, 35 pounds.

Three Single 4½-inch Burners

	Drilled or Sawed Burner
No. 703-B, Plain	$ 5.50
No. 703-B, Full Nickel	6.75

For Center Draft Burner Bowl add to list—701-B, 40 cents; 702-B, 80 cents; 703-B. $1.20.

In ordering, specify for Natural or Artificial Gas.

SERIES No. 720-B

(Same as No. 700-B)

Equipped with Giant and Simmering Burner   **Needle or Lever Valves**

One 4½-inch Single and One 5-inch Giant Burner with Simmering Burner

Weight crated, 26 pounds.

	Drilled or Sawed Burner
No. 722-B, Plain	$ 4.30
No. 722-B, Full Nickel	5.30

Two 4½-inch Single and One 5-inch Giant Burner with Simmering Burner

Weight crated, 36 pounds.

	Drilled or Sawed Burner
No. 723-B, Plain	$ 6.10
No. 723-B, Full Nickel	7.35

SERIES No. 7020-B

(Same as No. 700-B)

Equipped with Giant Double Burner   **Needle or Lever Valves**

One 4½-inch Single and One 5-inch Giant Double Burner

Weight crated, 26 pounds.

	Drilled or Sawed Burner
No. 7022-B, Plain	$ 4.45
No. 7022-B, Full Nickel	5.45

Two 4½-inch Single and One 5-inch Giant Double Burner

Weight crated, 36 pounds.

	Drilled or Sawed Burner
No. 7023-B, Plain	$ 6.25
No. 7023-B, Full Nickel	7.50

In ordering, specify for Natural or Artificial Gas.

SERIES No. 800

Reversible Grates, Raised or Flush
Removable Dirt Pans

Needle or Lever Valves

Size of Top, 12 x 12 inches.   Height, 6½ inches.   Weight crated, 15 pounds.
One Single 5-inch Burner

	Drilled or Sawed Burner
No. 801, Plain	$ 2.40
No. 801, Full Nickel	3.65

Size of Top, 12 x 25 inches.   Height, 6½ inches.   Weight crated, 30 pounds.
One Single 5-inch and One Single 4½-inch Burners

	Drilled or Sawed Burner
No. 802, Plain	$ 4.20
No. 802, Full Nickel	5.50

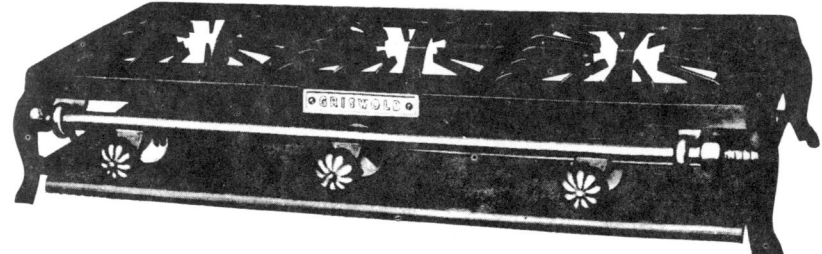

Size of Top, 12 x 35 inches.   Height, 6½ inches.   Weight crated, 38 pounds.
One Single 5-inch and Two Single 4½-inch Burners

	Drilled or Sawed Burner
No. 803, Plain	$ 6.00
No. 803, Full Nickel	7.75

In ordering, specify for Natural or Artificial Gas.

SERIES No. 8011

(Same as No. 800)

Reversible Grates, Raised or Flush   **Needle or Lever Valves**
Removable Dirt Pans

One 4½-inch Single and One 6-inch Jumbo Burner
Weight crated, 30 pounds.

	Drilled or Sawed Burner
No. 8012, Plain	$ 4.25
No. 8012, Full Nickel	5.75

Two 4½-inch Single and One 6-inch Jumbo Burner
Weight crated, 38 pounds.

	Drilled or Sawed Burner
No. 8013, Plain	$ 6.00
No. 8013, Full Nickel	8.00

SERIES No. 820

(Same as No. 800)

One 4½-inch Single and One 5-inch Giant with Simmering Burner
Weight crated, 30 pounds.

	Drilled or Sawed Burner
No. 822, Plain	$ 4.75
No. 822, Full Nickel	6.25

Two 4½-inch Single and One 5-inch Giant with Simmering Burner
Weight crated, 38 pounds.

	Drilled or Sawed Burner
No. 823, Plain	$ 6.50
No. 823, Full Nickel	8.50

SERIES No. 8020

(Same as No. 800)

One 4½inch Single and One 6¼-inch Giant Double Burner
Weight crated, 32 pounds.

	Drilled or Sawed Burner
No. 8022, Plain	$ 5.00
No. 8022, Full Nickel	6.50

Two 4½-inch Single and One 6¼-inch Giant Double Burner
Weight crated, 40 pounds.

	Drilled or Sawed Burner
No. 8023, Plain	$ 6.75
No. 8023, Full Nickel	8.75

In ordering, specify for Natural or Artificial Gas.

SERIES No. 900-B

Flush Grate Tops   **Needle or Lever Valves**

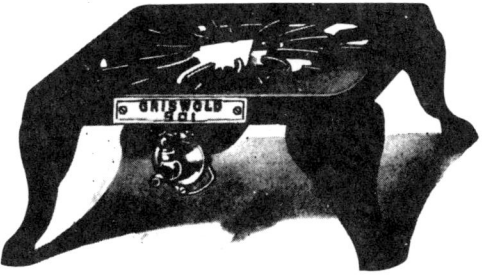

Size of Top, 12 x 12 inches.   Height, 6½ inches.   Weight crated, 14 pounds.
One Single 4½-inch Burner

	Drilled or Sawed Burner
No. 901-B, Plain	**$ 2.15**
No. 901-B, Full Nickel	**2.90**

Size of Top, 25 x 12 inches.   Height, 6½ inches.   Weight crated, 30 pounds.
Two Single 4½-inch Burners

	Drilled or Sawed Burner
No. 902-B, Plain	**$ 4.00**
No. 902-B, Full Nickel	**5.00**

Size of top, 35 x 12 inches.   Height, 6½ inches.   Weight crated, 38 pounds.
Three Single 4½-inch Burners

	Drilled or Sawed Burner
No. 903-B, Plain	**$ 5.60**
No. 903-B, Full Nickel	**6.85**

Dirt Pans can be furnished on above at net prices of 10 cents for one burner; 15 cents for two burners; 20 cents for three burners.

In ordering, specify for Natural or Artificial Gas.

SERIES No. 920-B

(Same as No. 900-B)

Equipped with Giant and Simmering Burner   **Needle or Lever Valves**

One 4½-inch Single and One 5-inch Giant Burner with Simmering Burner

Weight crated, 31 pounds.

	Drilled or Sawed Burner
No. 922-B, Plain	$ 4.60
No. 922-B, Full Nickel	5.60

Two 4½-inch Single and One 5-inch Giant Burner with Simmering Burner

Weight crated, 39 pounds.

	Drilled or Sawed Burner
No. 923-B, Plain	$ 6.20
No. 923-B, Full Nickel	7.45

SERIES No. 9020-B

(Same as No. 900-B)

Equipped with Giant Double Burner   **Needle or Lever Valves**

One 4½-inch Single and One 5-inch Giant Double Burner

Weight crated, 31 pounds.

	Drilled or Sawed Burner
No. 9022-B, Plain	$ 4.75
No. 9022-B, Full Nickel	5.75

Two 4½-inch Single and One 5-inch Giant Double Burner

Weight crated, 40 pounds.

	Drilled or Sawed Burner
No. 9023-B, Plain	$ 6.35
No. 9023-B, Full Nickel	7.60

Dirt pans can be furnished on above at net prices of 10 cents for one burner; 15 cents for two burners; 20 cents for three burners.

In ordering, specify for Natural or Artificial Gas.

SERIES No. 1000

Flush Grate Tops   **Slip Connection on No. 1001**

Needle or Lever Valves on Nos. 1002 and 1003

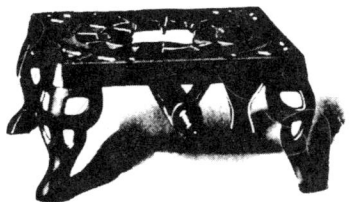

Size of Top, 8¼ x 8¼ inches.   Height, 4½ inches.   Weight crated, 5 pounds.

One Single 3½-inch Burner

	Loose Cap Burner	Drilled Burner
No. 1001, Plain	$ .75	$ .80
No. 1001, Full Nickel	1.25	1.30

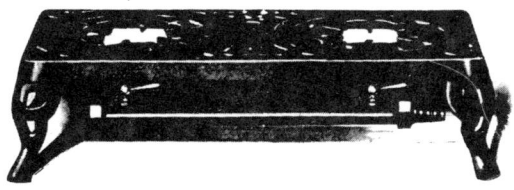

Size of Top, 8¼ x 17¼ inches.   Height, 4½ inches.   Weight crated, 12 pounds.

Two Single 3½-inch Burners

	Loose Cap Burner	Drilled Burner
No. 1002, Plain	$ 1.75	$1.85
No. 1002, Full Nickel	2.25	2.35

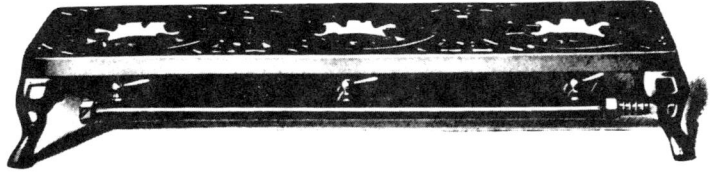

Size of Top, 8¼ x 26¼ inches.   Height, 4½ inches.   Weight crated, 17 pounds.

Three Single 3½-inch Burners

	Loose Cap Burner	Drilled Burner
No. 1003, Plain	$ 3.00	$ 3.15
No. 1003, Full Nickel	3.75	3.90

In ordering, specify for Natural or Artificial Gas.

ELEVATED HOT PLATES

One Pan Galvanized.   Frame well braced.

Needle or Lever Valves.   **Two Single 3½-inch Burners**

Size of Top, 20 x 10 inches.   Height, 24 inches.   Weight crated, 23 pounds.

Drilled or Sawed Burner

	Knocked Down	Set Up
No. 6020	$ 4.50	$ 5.10

Three Single 3½-inch Burners

Size of Top, 30 x 10 inches.   Height, 24 inches.   Weight crated, 30 pounds.

Drilled or Sawed Burner

	Knocked Down	Set Up
No. 6030	$ 6.00	$ 6.70

SERIES No. 6070-B

Needle or Lever Valves.   **Two Single 4½-inch Burners**

Size of Top, 23 x 11¾ inches.   Height, 24 inches.   Weight crated, 30 pounds.

Drilled or Sawed Burner

	Knocked Down	Set Up
No. 6072-B	$ 5.00	$ 5.60

Three Single 4½-inch Burners

Size of Top, 33 x 11¾ inches.   Height, 24 inches.   Weight Crated, 40 pounds.

Drilled or Sawed Burner

	Knocked Down	Set Up
No. 6073-B	$ 6.85	$ 7.55

These stoves are shipped knocked down unless otherwise specified.

In ordering, specify for Natural or Artificial Gas.

ELEVATED HOT PLATES

Has two Pans. Top pan galvanized iron, bottom pan japanned.

Needle or Lever Valves. **Two Single 4½-inch Burners.**

Size of Top, 23 x 11¾ inches. Height, 28 inches. Weight crated, 38 pounds.

Drilled or Sawed Burner

	Knocked Down	Set Up
No. 7020-B	**$ 5.50**	**$ 6.40**

Three Single 4½-inch Burners

Size of Top, 33 x 11¾ inches. Height, 28 inches. Weight crated, 50 pounds.

Drilled or Sawed Burner

	Knocked Down	Set Up
No. 7030-B	**$ 7.50**	**$ 8.50**

SERIES No. 7060

Needle or Lever Valves. **Two Single 3½-inch Burners.**

Size of Top, 20 x 10 inches. Height, 28 inches. Weight crated, 32 pounds.

Drilled or Sawed Burner

	Knocked Down	Set Up
No. 7062	**$ 5.00**	**$ 5.60**

Three Single 3½-inch Burners

Size of Top, 30 x 10 inches. Height, 28 inches. Weight crated, 45 pounds.

Drilled or Sawed Burner

	Knocked Down	Set Up
No. 7063	**$ 6.85**	**$ 7.55**

These stoves are shipped knocked down unless otherwise specified.

In ordering, specify for Natural or Artificial Gas.

EXTENSION TOP HOT PLATES

These Tops are made to be bolted on end of a Coal Range.

Needle or Lever Valves.

	Size of Top Inches	Weight Crated, Lbs.	Drilled or Sawed Burner
No. 752, Plain	22½ x 11¼	16	$ 3.40
No. 752, Nickel	22½ x 11¼	16	4.15
No. 753, Plain	32½ x 11¼	25	5.20
No. 753, Nickel	32½ x 11¼	25	6.20

In ordering, specify for Natural or Artificial Gas.

SKELETON GRATES

NURSERY

Dia. Burner, 3 inches
Dia. Plate, 5 inches   Height, 3 inches

7-inch Hot Plate Grates, per dozen	$2.25
8-inch Hot Plate Grates, per dozen	2.50
9-inch Hot Plate Grates, per dozen	3.00

No. 10, Plain	$ .50
No. 10, Nickel	1.00

In ordering, specify for Natural or Artificial Gas.

LAUNDRY STOVES

Needle or Lever Valves

	Size of Top Inches	Height Inches	Weight Crated, Lbs.	Drilled or Sawed Burner
No. 392, Two Burners	22 x 14	20½	53	**$ 8.75**
No. 393, Three Burners	32 x 14	20½	70	**11.25**
No. 394, Four Burners	22 x 22	20½	75	**13.65**

These stoves are made with closed tops for heating irons. The case is heavy sheet iron with lower shelf for flat irons, all finished in black japan.

Needle or Lever Valves

	Size of Top Inches	Height Inches	Weight Crated, Lbs.	Drilled or Sawed Burner
No. 212, Two Burners	25 x 12	19	40	**$ 5.00**
No. 213, Three Burners	35 x 12	19	50	**7.00**

In ordering, specify for Natural or Artificial Gas.

BURNERS

No. 1332
Loose Cap Burner
Diameter, 3½ inches.
Will fit Series No. 1000.

No. 1180-A
Loose Cap Burner
Diameter, 3½ inches.
Will fit Series No. 500.

No. 1916
Sawed Cap Burner
Diameter, 3½ inches.
Will fit Series No. 500.

No. 1915
Drilled Cap Burner
Diameter, 3½ inches.
Will fit Series Nos. 500 and 1000.

No. 1149
Drilled Burner
Diameter, 3½ inches.
Will fit Series No. 600.

No. 1151
Sawed Burner
Diameter, 3½ inches.
Will fit Series No. 600.

No. 674
Drilled Burner
Diameter, 4½ inches.
Will fit Series Nos. 700-B, 800, 900-B,
7000-B, 8000, 9000-B.

No. 676
Sawed Burner
Diameter, 4½ inches.
Will fit Series Nos. 700-B, 800, 900-B,
7000-B, 8000, 9000-B.

No. 677
Drilled Giant Burner
Diameter, 5 inches.
Will fit Series |Nos.
700-B, 900-B, 800.

No. 678
Sawed Giant Burner
Diameter, 5 inches.
Will fit Series Nos.
700-B, 900-B, 800.

No. 677 with No. 681
Drilled Giant Burner with Simmering Burner
Diameter, 5 inches.
Will fit Series Nos. 700-B, 900-B, 800.

No. 678 with No. 681
Sawed Giant Burner with Simmering Burner
Diameter, 5 inches.
Will fit Series Nos. 700-B, 900-B, 800.

No. 677 with No. 679
Drilled Double Burner
Diameter, 5 inches.
Will fit Series Nos. 7000-B, 9000-B.

No. 678 with No. 680
Sawed Double Burner
Diameter, 5 inches.
Will fit Series Nos. 7000-B, 9000-B.

No. 1666
Drilled Jumbo Burner
Diameter, 6 inches.
Will fit Series No. 800, 7000-B, 9000-B.

No. 1667
Sawed Jumbo Burner
Diameter, 6 inches.
Will fit Series N0. 800, 7000-B, 9000-B.

No. 1691
Drilled Double Burner
Diameter, 6¼ inches, with 3-inch Center Burner.
Will fit Series No. 800.

No. 1692
Sawed Double Burner
Diameter, 6¼ inches with 3-inch Center Burner.
Will fit Series No. 800.

No. 1788-D
Drilled Burner
Diameter, 4½ inches.
Will fit Series No. 100.

No. 1788-S
Sawed Burner
Diameter, 4½ inches.
Will fit Series No. 100.

No. 1787-D
Drilled Double Burner
Diameter, 6½ inches.
Will fit Series No. 100.

No. 1787-S
Sawed Double Burner
Diameter, 6½ inches.
Will fit Series No. 100.

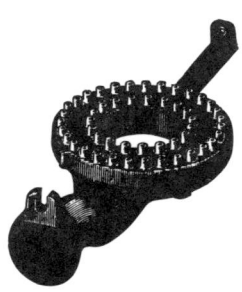

No. 1147
Drilled Burner
Diameter, 4½ inches.
Will fit Series No. 300.

No. 1148
Sawed Burner
Diameter, 4½ inches.
Will fit Series No. 300.

No. 1143
Drilled Burner
Diameter, 4½ inches.
Will fit Series No. 200.

No. 1145
Sawed Burner
Diameter, 4½ inches.
Will fit Series No. 200.

OVENS FOR GAS, GASOLINE, ALCOHOL AND OIL STOVES

BULLETIN
NUMBER O-2-B

THE GRISWOLD MFG. CO.
ERIE, PENNSYLVANIA, U. S. A.

S-7-108

GRISWOLD BOLO OVENS.

For Gas, Gasoline, Alcohol and Oil Stoves.

TERMS.

Sixty days or two per cent discount for cash, if paid within 10 days from date of invoice.

All bills payable in New York or other par funds without allowance for exchange.

No charge for crating or cartage.

No freight allowance on shipments weighing less than 200 pounds. Positively no deviation from this rule.

We take special care in the packing of our goods. Every piece carefully packed, insuring against breakage.

After goods are shipped in good order our liability ceases, and we cannot allow any claim for breakage or other damage in transit.

Claims for errors or deficiences will not be entertained unless made within FIVE DAYS after receipt of goods.

GRISWOLD BOLO OVENS.

For Gas, Gasoline, Alcohol and Oil Stoves.

"BOLO" means "Big Oven," "Little Oven"—two in one. The only real improvement ever made in Portable Ovens. An oven that cuts the cost of operating in half, with better results.

The big feature of the "BOLO" is a Removable Air Circulating Chamber that changes the "Big Oven" to a "Little Oven" in two seconds reducing space to half, baking in half the time, with half the gas.

The only Oven that will bake FAST and SLOW at the same time. The circulation is perfect.

Double Walls. Rolled Edge Doors, which fit into rabbited joint frame, like the door of a refrigerator, keeping the heat inside and cold air outside.

Made in two sizes. Glass or solid doors. The glass is well tempered, and will not break easily.

All "BOLO" Ovens are full tin lined and equipped with electrically welded racks.

Oven bottom plates are made of No. 22 guage iron. Closed all around the sides and flush with the opening at the door so that crumbs and dirt may be brushed out.

Nickel plated steel hinges, with mica windows, nickel plated stamped steel corner pieces on a japanned extension top and Always-Cold wood handles.

The interior of glass door oven is always visible. Roasts or baking can be watched without opening the door. Saves time and prevents cooling or jarring of delicate cakes.

We guarantee all Ovens. Prices and terms gladly furnished.

THE GRISWOLD MFG. CO.,
Erie, Penna., U. S. A.

GRISWOLD BOLO OVENS.

The above illustration shows the taken down parts and other exclusive features of the "BOLO" Oven.

First. The Circulating Air Chamber. When the sliding section is placed at the top, the full inside space may be used. When placed in midway lining groove the lower half may be used for quick baking and the upper compartment for slow roasting, baking or warming closet.

Second. Showing side lining groove in which the movable section slides and humps to prevent putting in any but the right place.

Third. Electrically welded racks.

Fourth. Japanned extension top, nickeled corner pieces. It also shows the rabbited door joint. Rolled edge door. Set screws and wire guards for glass oven door. Wood handles. Nickeled steel hinges, with mica windows and door catch, found only on Griswold "BOLO" Ovens.

Patents, covering the various inventions, applied for.

GRISWOLD BOLO OVENS.

No. 60-B

No. 80-B

Removable Circulating Air Chamber.

Made of polished steel. Rolled edge door. Rabbited joint door frame. Full tin lined. Wood handles. Steel nickel plated hinge and catch. Nickel plated corner pieces. Perfect ventilation.

No.	Height.	Width.	Depth.	Wt. Crated.	List.
60-B	18½ in.	14 in.	13½ in.	22 lbs.	**$5.20**
80-B	18½ in.	20 in.	13½ in.	27 lbs.	**$5.70**

GRISWOLD BOLO OVENS.

No. 160-B
Size of Glass in Door, 8½x9 inches.

No. 180-B
Size of Glass in Door, 9x15 inches.

Removable Circulating Air Chamber.

Made of polished steel. Rolled edge door. Rabbited joint door frame. Full tin lined. Wood handles. Steel nickel plated hinge and catch. Nickel plated corner pieces. Perfect ventilation.

No.	Height.	Width.	Depth.	Wt. Crated.	List.
160-B	18½ in.	14 in.	13½ in.	23 lbs.	**$5.60**
180-B	18½ in.	20 in.	13½ in.	28 lbs.	**$6.20**

"BOLO" Ovens have been thoroughly tried and tested by the best Domestic Science experts in America on all kinds of baking under all conditions. We are confident we can prove our claim for economical, gas saving, perfect baking ovens. So confident, we will gladly send you one on approval; all charges prepaid for a try-out at your own store or home and will pay all charges back to our factory if you are not satisfied our claims are justified.

Every woman who comes into your store will want to see the "BOLO" Oven and the economical features, for they have already read about them in the leading women's magazines.

Show them the Removable Circulating Air Chamber and how the lower compartment will heat in half the time when quick baking is necessary. Show them how slow roasting and quick baking may be accomplished at the same time, by placing the slow roasting or baking in upper compartment, while quick baking, such as biscuit or pies, are baked in the lower. No other oven is made in which this operation can be accomplished successfully.

Show them the rolled edge doors that will not warp out of shape and the rabbited joint door frame. Flush oven bottom is most important feature not found in other ovens.

Meter tests show a difference of 40 to 50 per cent. of heat between the lower and upper compartments of the "BOLO" Oven, thus showing the actual saving of gas.

Call their attention to the many special features in the make up of "BOLO" Ovens and your sale is made with a handsome profit and a satisfied customer, which is success to any dealer.

Order a sample line of "BOLO" Ovens and be prepared to meet the demand created by our special advertising. We will refer all inquiries to the nearest dealer.

GAS HEATERS

BULLETIN
NUMBER H-6

THE GRISWOLD MFG. CO.
ERIE, PENNSYLVANIA, U. S. A.

S-8-115

GRISWOLD GAS HEATING STOVES

Have been on the market so long and are so well known that the question of quality cannot be disputed.

We use the best material and labor that money can buy. Should a **GRISWOLD** heater fall short of your expectations, we are here to make good any of our claims. Our guarantee goes with the stoves. Being located in the heart of the natural gas territory where gas heating stoves are the principal means of heating, we have by many years experience succeeded in making gas heaters as near perfect as possible.

The principle of burning is one of the oldest. Efficiency of a gas heater depends on its power to produce a given temperature in a specified time on the least consumption of gas.

GRISWOLD GAS HEATERS increase the efficiency of gas as a fuel because they release all the heat units.

To those who have never experienced the many advantages in selling this line, we respectfully solicit a sample order, and to the customers who have, we can only say we will continue to build the best gas heater of its class that money can buy.

THE
GRISWOLD MANUFACTURING COMPANY,
Erie, Pennsylvania, U. S. A.

GRISWOLD GAS HEATERS

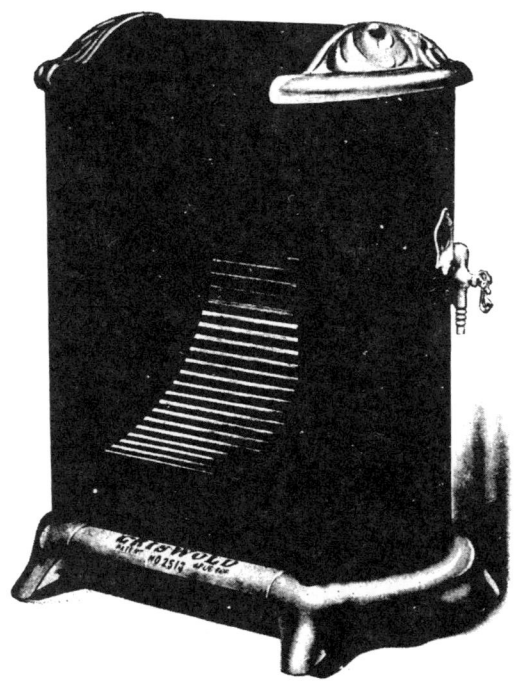

No. 2500 Series Reflector

Body made of patented planished iron.

Inside back and sides made of pure 10 oz. copper, highly polished.

Burner is fitted with lava tips made in Germany especially for our stoves.

Valve is adjustable control, a special design of our own, combining a ¼-inch pipe connection and hose nipple.

No.	Height Inches	Width Inches	Depth Inches	Tips to Burner	Consume Per Hour Feet	Weight Crated Lbs.	Price List Nickel Top	Price List Full Nickel
2511	23	17	11½	12	10	28½	$5.40	$ 6.15
2513	24	19	11½	15	12	30	6.25	7.00
2516	25	22	11½	19	18	31½	7.75	8.50
2519	26	25	11½	23	20	33	9.25	10.00

No.	Guards List	No.	Guards List
2511	$0.55	2516	$0.65
2513	.60	2519	.70

The oval ends give a larger flue, drawing the cold air from the floor, making a more efficient heater than any other make.

Note—For vessel water heater or hot plate attachment see page eleven.

GRISWOLD GAS HEATERS

No. 500 Series. Reflector

Copper reflector back. Illuminating flame. Nickel trimmings. Polished steel case. Fitted with flue connections.

Burner is fitted with lava tips made in Germany especially for our stoves.

Valve is adjustable control, a special design of our own, combining a ¼-inch pipe connection and hose nipple.

No.	Height Inches	Width Inches	Depth Inches	Tips to Burner	Consume Per Hour Feet	Weight Crated Pounds	Price List
509	19	9	8½	8	8	12	$ 3.00
510	23	10	9	11	10	14	4.00
513	24½	13	9	15	12	20	6.00
516	26½	16	9	19	18	21	7.50
519	28½	19	9	23	20	24	9.00
522	28½	22	9	27	24	26	10.50
526	28½	26	9	33	30	28	12.00

No. 509 has hose nipple connection; no flue connection.

GRISWOLD GAS HEATER DRESS GUARDS

The above cut shows heater fitted with improved dress guard. It is so made that clothing cannot come in contact with flame. The guard is easily attached or detached by means of spring wire at the side.

No.	Guards List Price Each
509	$0.50
510	.55
513	.60
516	.65
519	.70
522	.75
526	.90

GRISWOLD GAS HEATERS

No. 300

Cast Base and Top. Polished Steel Drum.

Cast Blue Flame Burner with adjustable air mixer for natural gas, or six-arm Brass Star Burner for artificial gas. (See page 11 for illustration of Burners).

Top is fitted with concealed flue connection. (See page 10).

No.	Height Inches	Diameter of Drum Inches	Diameter of Base Inches	Weight Crated Lbs.	Black or Aluminum List	Nickel or Antique Copper List
300	23¾	8½	12	21	$4.00	$5.00

In ordering, specify whether Blue Flame Burner or Brass Star Burner is wanted, and if for Natural or Artificial Gas.

GRISWOLD GAS HEATERS

No. 150

Cast Base and Top. Polished Steel Drum. Fitted with a Cast Blue Flame Burner with adjustable air mixer or six-arm Brass Star Burner (shown on page 11).

Top is fitted with a concealed flue connection. (See page 10).

No.	Height Inches	Diameter of Drum Inches	Diameter of Base Inches	Weight Crated Lbs.	Black or Aluminum List	Nickel or Antique Copper List
150	20¼	7	10¼	13	$3.00	$3.50

In ordering, state if for Natural or Artificial Gas.

GRISWOLD GAS HEATERS

No. 100

Cast Base and Top. Polished Steel Drum. Fitted with a Cast Blue Flame Burner with adjustable air mixer or six-arm Brass Star Burner, illuminating flame (shown on page 11). Top is fitted with concealed flue connection (see page 10).

No.	Height Inches	Diameter of Drum Inches	Diameter of Base Inches	Weight Crated Lbs.	Black or Aluminum List	Nickel or Antique Copper List
100	18¼	7	10¼	13	$2.50	$3.00

In ordering, state if for Natural or Artificial Gas.

GRISWOLD GAS HEATERS

Victor No. 0

Cast Base and Top. Polished Steel Drum. Fitted with a six-arm Brass Star Burner, or Loose Cap Cast Blue Flame Burner (shown on page 11).

No.	Height	Diameter of Drum Inches	Diameter of Base Inches	Weight Crated Lbs.	Plain Black List	Aluminum List	Nickel List
0	18	6	9¾	10	$2.00	$2.10	2.50

In ordering, state if for Natural or Artificial Gas.

GRISWOLD GAS HEATERS

Concealed Flue Connection fitted on our
Nos. 100, 150 and 300

This cut shows the **GRISWOLD** Drum Heater with flue attached. This feature is especially desirable, not only as a means to carry off the disagreeable odor which comes from a stove without a flue, but is a strong talking point in selling where City ordinances compel dealers to sell stoves with flue connections only.

The pipe collar is completely concealed under top when not needed. The Cast Blue Flame Burner is one of the most powerful for heating.

The combustion is perfect, making the **GRISWOLD** Drum Heaters more efficient than many heaters of twice the size.

DRUM HEATER BURNERS

No. 686

This cut shows the style of Blue Flame Burner used in our Nos. 300, 150 and 100 Drum Heaters. This Burner is drilled and fitted with nickel air mixer giving a perfect blue flame.

This cut shows the Brass Arm Star Burner used in our Nos. 300, 150, 100 and 0 Drum Heaters. It is the best constructed Brass Star Burner made; the arms are seamless brass tubes, screwed in a solid cast head. The Burner is drilled for illuminating flame, five jets in each arm and is fitted for either gas.

Note—When ordering, specify for what number of stove Star Burner is needed.

No. 666

This cut shows the Loose Cap Cast Blue Flame Burner used in our No. 0 Drum Heater.

No. 1142

Vessel Water Heater or Hot Plate attachment for our No. 2500 series heater. It is cast in one piece. Easily placed in position for service. Simply place it over oval top of stove. See illustration of Oval Reflector Heater on page three.

1996 Price Guide

Prices are for **EACH** item number listed under the corresponding pictures.

1ST SECTION – Bulletin No. A-9

Page 4 – Coffee Pot	$60-75
Tea Pot	$65-80
Page 5 – Perkolator	$110-130
Page 6 – Tea Pot	$90-110
Five O'clock Tea	$110-120
Page 7 – Double Boiler	$75-90
Col. Flt Btm. Tea	$70-80
Page 8 – "Safety First"	
Colonial Tea Kettle	$50-70
Page 9 – Flt. Btm. Tea	$70-90
"The Rapid" . . .	
Corgtd. Btm. Tea	$80-95
Page 10 – Water Pitcher	$140-160
Bail Water Pitch.	$90-110
Page 11 – Skillet (wood hdle)	$75-100
Skillet	$80-110
Page 12 – Shallow Skillet	$75-100
Oyster Pan	$100-125
Page 13 – Handle Griddle	$80-100
Bailed Griddle	$75-90
Page 14 – Long Griddle	$75-95
Berlin Sauce Pan	$70-90
Page 15 – Berlin Boiler	$65-85
Berlin Sauce Pan	$70-90
Page 16 – All on this page	$30-50
Page 17 – All on this page	$40-60
Page 18 – Roaster/Dutch Oven	$60-80
Oval Roaster	$150-200
Page 19 – Waffle Mold	$50-75
Deep Ring Waf. Mold	$60-80
Page 20 – Shirred Egg Dish	$20-40
Pudding Pan	$30-50
Casserole	$40-60
Page 21 – Omelet Fry Pan	$75-100
Flop Griddle	$200-300
Bread Stick Pan	$60-80
Page 22 – Gem/Muffin Top	$60-80
Gem/Muffin Mid.	$60-80
Golf Ball Gem	$75-95
Page 23 – All on this page	$60-80

2ND SECTION – Bulletin No. E-5

Page 4 – Iron Hdl. Skillet #3-10	$20-40
#11-14	$50-75
Wood Hdl. #3-6, 11-12	$100-150
#7-8	$50-70
Page 5 – Shallow Skillet	$100-135
Deep Skillet	$70-120
Page 6 – Iron Hdl. Griddle	$40-60
Wood Hdl. Griddle	$100-135
Page 7 – All on this page	$75-125
Page 8 – Long Griddle	$50-75
N. England Griddle	$140-225
Page 9 – All on this page	$200-300
Page 10 – Scotch Bowl	$90-110
Yankee Bowl	$60-75
Page 11 – Top Dutch Ovens	$60-80
Btm. Dutch Ovens w/legs	
#8, 9, 12	$250-300
#10-11	$150-175
#13	$350-400
Page 12 – Maslin Shaped Kettle	
#4-6, 8	$50-70
#12	$100-120
Flat Btm. Kettle	
#6-8	$80-100
#9-10	$100-120
Page 13 – Low Kettle	$40-60
Regular Kettle	$65-75
Page 14 – All on this page	$65-85
Page 15 – Low Ecc. Kettle	$60-80
Eccentric Kettle	$70-80
Page 16 – Eccentric B. Pot	$90-110
Lg. Ecc. Pot	$100-120
Page 17 – Oval Roaster	$200-300
Ham Boiler	$400-500
Page 18 – Victor Skillet	$40-55
Tea Kettle	$175-225
Page 19 – Coffee Roaster	$1000+
Apple/Danish Pan	$90-110
Plett Pan	$40-60
Page 20 – Gem Pans #1	$100-150
Gem Pan #3	$150-190
Gem Pan #5 & 6	$150-175
Gem Pan #8	$70-90
Gem Pan #9	$90-110

CONTINUED

6TH Section – Bulletin No. R-8

Page 9 – Hot Plates Series No. 700-B

#701-B	$100-125
#702-B	$100-125
#703-B	$125-150

Page 11 – Hot Plates Series No. 800

#801	$100-125
#802	$100-125
#803	$125-150

Page 13 – Hot Plates Series No. 900-B

#901-B	$100-125
#902-B	$100-125
#903-B	$125-150

Page 15 – Hot Plates Series No. 1000

#1001	$100-125
#1002	$100-125
#1003	$125-150

Page 16 – Elevated Hot Plates – $150-200

Page 17 – Elevated Hot Plates – $150-200

Page 18 – Extension Hot Plate – $100-125
Nursery Hot Plate $50-75

Page 19 – Laundry Stove

#392, 393, 394	$100-150
#212, 213	$75-100

All Pages 20-23 – Burners are all – $25+

Page 11 – Drum Heater Burners

#686	$25+
2nd picture	$15+
#666	$15+
#1142	$10+

7TH SECTION – Bulletin No. O-2-B

Page 5 – Bolo Oven #60-B $65-90
Bolo Oven #80-B $100-125

Page 6 – Bolo Oven #160-B $75-100
Bolo Oven #180-B $125-140

8TH SECTION – Bulletin No. H-6

Page 3 – Gas Heater #2500 Series – $150-175

Page 4 – Gas Heater #500 Series – $150-175

Page 5 – Gas Heater Dress Guards – $15+

Page 6 – Gas Heater #300 $150-175

Page 7 – Gas Heater #150 $150-175

Page 8 – Gas Heater #100 $150-175

Page 9 – Gas Heater #0 $150-175